THE Whisperers

SPARKIE WILSON

BALBOA.PRESS

A DIVISION OF HAY HOUSE

Balboa Press books may be ordered through booksellers or by contacting:

Balboa Press
A Division of Hay House
1663 Liberty Drive
Bloomington, IN 47403
www.balboapress.com
844-682-1282

Print information available on the last page.

ISBN: 978-1-9822-5342-4 (sc)
ISBN: 978-1-9822-5343-1 (e)

Balboa Press rev. date: 09/30/2020

Table of Contents

New Orleans

Odd Left Overs

Bowling Green

My Imaginary Friend

When I was a little girl, before I went to school, I could see and talk to my Guardian Angel. I use to know his name, but that has been lost with time. I called him my friend because he was the only friend I ever had growing up. In my stories I call him Angel.

When it was my turn to set the table, I always set a place for him at the table. Next to me of course. When I first started doing this, Daddy looked at me.

"Baby, what are you doing? Are we having company I don't know about?"

"Yes, Daddy, my friend is coming to eat with me."

He let it slide. I am positive that he thought I would grow out of it before it drove him crazy. Well, as it happened, it drove him crazy long before I was ready to stop. After a while I was told not to set the table, my sister would do that.

"Sherry, don't forget a place for my friend, please." She just laughed at me.

"Daddy told me to set the table because of your invisible friend crazy."

"He is not invisible, I see him."

"Really what is he wearing then? Does he have white wings?"

"No he doesn't have wings. He has a black coat that's long and black pants, and a really nice smile. He makes me laugh."

"Good grief, you talk to him and he talks back?"

"Yes, why?" She was whispering now.

"Don't tell anyone that! They will put you away and you will never get out."

"Where would they put me?"

"In a hospital that you would not like, and they will do terrible things to you."

"Why would they do that sissy?"

"Because you would be crazy."

"How do you know this?"

"Because I heard them talking about a girl at school that had to go to the crazy hospital. They made her shock. I don't know what that is but it's not good."

"Hay girls what are you whispering about? You look really serious. What are we discussing?" Mama, never asked questions she didn't know the answer to. We both said at the same time "About how there are only 4 plates on the table from now on."

"Good." She walked off shaking her head. Sherry gave me a hug.

I didn't talk about him after that. I was sure I didn't want to shock. It made me sad, but then Angel told me it was ok, he wasn't everybody's friend. He was mine and it didn't hurt his feelings. He would sit on the floor next to me. That's what he did.

We had moved across town when I was three. We are moving to a new house! I get to take my kitten, Sleepy with me. I held her on my lap as we drive to the new house in Daddy's car.

"Oh my! This sure is a big white house Daddy! OH, it has a porch that goes all around it with four big white columns! It even has a place to put your car Daddy!" Daddy was smiling. I get out of the car and look up. It was so tall, I couldn't see the top of it. Oh and it had steps, real steps that go right up to the porch. Sleepy and I go up the steps to the porch. We were slow at first. Sherry runs past me, cause she is always faster than me and my big sister is always in a hurry. We walk inside. The house is huge inside too!

"Daddy where will I sleep with Sleepy?"

"Well Tadpole, in this house you have your own room." I wasn't sure I liked that. He saw the frown on my face. Sherry and I always shared a room.

"Come with me and I will show you where it is." He took my hand and we walked down a dark hallway. I didn't like the dark hallway, it scared me. I held Daddy's hand tight. We went past Sherry's room. I waved at her, she laughed at me. Finally; we were in my room.

"Oh Daddy, it has a big window and lots of sunshine. We love it!" I said as I hugged Sleepy. Her bed was right next to mine; she will not need it though. My bed was right next to the huge window, so when I took my nap I could look out the window. Daddy left and I went to the door to leave.....but that hallway was dark. So, I stayed in my room. I liked it here, it was really sunny! I could hear people bringing in furniture and talking. There was a lot going on, but I couldn't go down that dark hallway, it was scary! After a while I started to get hungry. I decided I needed to be brave like The Shadow. Angel and I ran as fast as we could down that hall.

Wow, the whole place had changed! It wasn't empty now and it looked like home. All of the things that I loved were here now. What a great place! I went into the kitchen.

"Daddy, can I have a sandwich? I'm hungry."

I went out the front door with my PB&J sandwich. Sherry was already outside. She and I were outside exploring the yard. The grass made my feet tingle. I loved this place. Then I heard someone calling me from the big open windows next door.

"Oh little girl, Oh little girl."

I walked over to the edge of the yard. I looked up at the big windows and saw the sweetest face I had ever seen. She had the face of a fairy godmother. The sweet woman said "What's your name little girl?"

"My name is Debbe but everybody calls me Sparkie. What is your name Lady?"

"Well I'm your new neighbor."

So you can understand how the confusion was caused by this. I believed her name was Neighbor and that's what I called her. She handed me a plate of cookies out the window and we became fast friends.

School took Sherry away all day, so I would go see Neighbor with my angel. She couldn't see him of course but she talked to him and set a place for him at the table when we had tea. In the summer we would have lemonade and in the winter we would have hot chocolate. She always put out three glasses or mugs.

"I don't think he can drink it Sparkie, but it just doesn't seem polite not to serve him as well."

I loved Neighbor. For months and months, we had tea parties and played games and visited. Always at Neighbors house, sometimes with Sleepy, who was getting big now; but always with Angel. Just about every day. Mama didn't seem to mind us going over there and I was happy to have another friend.

One day Neighbor came to my house with Angel! She could see him and they were talking. She looked so happy and younger. She had come into my room to visit me while I was taking a nap. This was strange, because she never came to my house. I sat up when she and Angel came in. She sat down on my bed and gave me a big hug.

"Sparkie, I came to tell you that most people don't understand how everything works. You are a very lucky little girl to have me and your angel as your friends." I knew she was right.

"I can't visit long, but I want you to know that I love you very much. You will be able to see me anytime, but nobody else will. Awww, honey don't cry. I know you will be strong, because I am very happy. I have to go away and I will not be your neighbor any more. But you need me just call for me I will come back. Ok? You will always have Angel." She gave me another hug.

"But why do you have to go? I don't want you to go."

"I know, but I promise I will always be around."

"I don't understand."

"I know you don't know now, but one day you will be big enough to understand. I promise."

I looked at Angel, 'What is going on? Why does Neighbor have to go away? Where is she going?"

"The circle of life is going on."

I just looked at him and nodded my head.

We were in my room. Then I heard my Grandmother in the kitchen talking to my mother. We moved down the hallway so I could hear what they were saying.

"No Chelcie, Debbe is too young to see dead bodies."

"She really likes Dr. Keith's mother. She is over there all the time. Why yesterday she visited her. How did she die?"

"She went peacefully in her sleep. She didn't suffer and really didn't have any health problems. Debbe needs to go see what life is all about. This might shake the invisible friend right out of her."

"I don't think that's a problem, she doesn't talk about him anymore. We don't have a place for him at the table either."

"Well I have talked to Earl and he says that I can take her, so I am taking her."

That's weird, Mama rarely stuck up for me. Then Grandmother called me.

"Debbe Jean! Get in here." I looked at Angel and Neighbor.

"We will go with you don't worry baby."

Grandmother only used both of my names when she was mad at me about something I did. I walked into the kitchen and Grandmother grabbed me by the hand and started walking me to Neighbors house. My other hand was holding tight to Neighbors hand and Angel was smiling. Grandmother picked me up and carried me up the stairs to the porch. She said I was too slow. I started to tell her I could climb them, but Neighbor smiled and put her pointer finger over her mouth for me to be quite. So I didn't say anything. She carried me into the house, I never let go of Neighbor's hand.

We walked up to the coffin and there was a woman that looked like Neighbor but something was missing. Grandmother was saying something about Neighbor being gone and that she would not be here for me to visit. I just nodded.

"What do you think? How does she look?" Grandmother said.

"Well she doesn't look very happy." When I said that Neighbor and Angel started laughing, so I did too.

"Mercy child she's dead, she's not supposed to look happy! Get down, go home. I'm staying here a while."

Wow gladly, I got down. I had Neighbor's hand and Angel took my other hand and the three of us walked down the stairs for the last time together and back to my house.

Neighbor gave me a hug and a kiss.

"Sparkie, I love you. You know if you need me all you have to do is call, right?"

"Yes ma'am, I know. I love you too."

And then she was gone. My angel put his arm across my shoulders and we walked into the house. Mama was on the phone so we just went back to my room. I never called for Neighbor, Angel said she was happy and as long as he was there I was happy too.

Aunt Sadie

When I was four going on five years old, I had developed a wart on my right thumb. I rubbed it constantly and I was again driving my parents' crazy. They had tried all of the over the counter products on the market at the time to get rid of warts. You have to remember that it is now 1955. There really was not a lot of over the counter medicines to be found, like today. They had also tried a lot of ole wives' tale remedies, they did not work either. Mama was sure I got it because I was always outside in the woods and brought home numerous strange things including frogs. I played with frogs, I didn't believe they caused warts. I like them.

One sunny Saturday I was getting ready to go to the woods; when my Daddy said, "Tadpole, come here, we are going into town." Humm that was strange. We never went into town, just the two of us. Wonder if that was what Mama was talking about when she said "I would not be caught dead with that woman. You want to go fine and take her with you, but I am never going there."

We pulled up in front of a yellow house with what use to be white trim by the creek. Oh No! I know this place. We come here and get worms when we would go fishing. Worms huh, they were little snakes. Bigger than my thumb most of them. I wouldn't touch them. We always came to get them at night, with a flashlight. Went down to the creek and flipped over some nasty material, and the ground looked like it was alive with them! Wiggling all over each other and Daddy would reach down and pick up a wiggling hand full of them and put them in a coffee can. YUCK! I finally got where I would just dig my own worms at home. They were little like me and I had a coffee can too. After the first time and I screamed, Daddy didn't care if I stayed in the car, I was so scared of them! But it's daytime. What are we doing here? I picked at the wart unconsciously. Daddy reached over and put his big hand on mine. "It's ok tadpole, we are not here for night crawlers." "Good, cause I wasn't going to go down there even in the daytime." Daddy laughed.

He opened my door and picked me up. He knew I was nervous. "I can walk Daddy, just hold my hand." We walked hand and hand through the grown up yard. Lots of weeds and huge trees. I liked the trees, they were old and friendly. We got to the back of the house. It was creepy. We went up two of the old wooden steps that went to a kind of room. Daddy said it was a screened in porch. "Aunt Sadie? You home?"

The screen door to the house creaked open just a crack.

"Whatch ya want Earl"?" Came a low gravelly voice. It matched the house. Creepy!

"I was just checking on you. I got Debbe with me. Thought you might want to see her." ME! Why would that person want to see me?

"Bring her closer so I can get a look at the little thing." Little thing?? Maybe she couldn't tell I was a little girl? I had braids, that should be a hint. Daddy nudged me. NO way was I going any closer to her. Nope, sure not. Daddy picked me up. He carried me inside the porch and sat me down on the floor. Well, that was helpful. I started looking around, there was everything you could ever imagine in there. Including wasps, spiders, and mice. I had just started looking around. Boxes of anything you might imagine. Lots of stuff, I had no idea what most of it was, but it looked interesting. I was so engrossed in what I was looking at that I didn't see Daddy leave! He was gone! So was Aunt Sadie. They were inside the house;

I could hear them talking. There was a window that was open so I went to listen under the window. They were quiet at first, I could not understand what they were saying, but then the yelling started and I understood all of it.

"No, I will not take it. I will not and you can't make me. I don't care if that decision will hurt me. I am not taking it." Then it got quiet again, the talking didn't stop, it was just real low. Then I heard, "Well why is you here then, if it aint for the family gift?"

"Oh, I uh, brought Debbe, she plays with frogs and is always out in the woods. She brings home all sorts of critters. She has a wart on her right thumb, we have tried everything, but it will not go away. I just thought you might charm it off." What was he doing? What was charming, if she did it I don't like it. Look at this creepy place. Wonder if she is going to keep me here? I will run away, first chance. Where was Angel, he didn't come with me for the first time ever. This place has to be bad if he will not come here. (My guardian Angel was always with me. I use to know His name, but I don't remember it anymore, so I call Him Angel in these stories.)

"She's the one with the invisible friend right?"

"Yes, how did you know that?"

Again it was too quiet.

"Ok, since Dr. Moore's mother passed, she has been acting strange. Not really herself. She hasn't mentioned her invisible friend lately either, she doesn't make a place for him at the table either. So I am pretty sure we are through that phase of her childhood." I wondered what a phase was and how you get one or lose one, or go through one, I don't remember going through anything lately. I guess I had though if Daddy said so.

"Really, you don't find that a bit odd Earl? Maybe Neighbor is with her all the time now?"

"Shut up! How did you know she called Dr. Moore's mother Neighbor?" Daddy must really be mad, cause you are not supposed to say shut up, that what he tells me.

"Is she talking more or less now."

"Less and she stays outside or in her room. She doesn't come around the family much, unless we go get her and then she isn't happy about it."

"And you think all that is normal?"

"She is 4 almost 5. She is fine. She eats well, sings and plays with her cat.

"She has a cat not a dog? What is the cats name?"

"Sleepy."

"Where is she I thought you said she was here."

"She is still on the porch."

"Oh no, no, no!"

Well that scared me and I stopped in mid step. What was out here? Something that could eat me? I had found the Halloween decorations. I loved Halloween. They were soo cool. Real looking bats, snake skins, strange things in bottles. Even an eye looking at me. I was having the best time ever. I even found a hat to put on and an old black robe. YAY! What else was here? Just as I was reaching for the stick that I could smack things with, my feet were off the ground! Aunt Sadie had picked me up and started taking things away from me. She wasn't mad. She was just quick. "You can keep the hat baby; it looks good on you." I gave it back anyway when Daddy frowned and shook his head no. She was even scary when she was happy. She was smiling now.

"Aunt Sadie, can we borrow some of your decorations at Halloween?" She let out a laugh that made me laugh. It didn't have the same effect on Daddy though, he wasn't laughing.

"You sure could precious if your Daddy says so, but I don't believe he will like that one little bit." Daddy! I had forgotten all about Daddy. Where was he? Why had he left me? I couldn't see him anymore.

"Aunt Sadie, is going to make your wart go away, Tadpole. That will be nice right?" I heard Daddy say that but I couldn't see him. I never knew what was wrong with my wart anyway. I just nodded my head.

"Earl, you go on now, either inside or outside, but you can't stay here." Daddy went into the house. I heard him sit down. We were still by the window and everything in her house creaked.

"Ok baby, where is this wart that is bothering you."

"Aunt Sadie, it doesn't bother me, it bothers Mama and Daddy. I kinda like it."

"Well we can't have them upset. Show Aunt Sadie where it is."

I held out my right thumb as we went back to the Halloween decorations. She sat down in a rocking chair and I was standing in between her legs. I had my left hand on her leg resting it there. She reached over and pulled out a black needle that had black thread in it.

"Aunt Sadie, I have never seen a black needle, that is so awesome, where did you get it? I'd like to have one."

She just smiled and started humming and rocking. In just a few minutes she said something I didn't understand, she had both of her hands on my head. I started humming the song too. I love music. She kissed the top of my head and then took my thumb, and with the black needle she said something again and put the needle into the wart and drew the black thread through the wart.

"There you are baby girl. That wart will be gone in a day or two." She gave me a big hug like Neighbor use to.

"Aunt Sadie, you don't have to worry about Neighbor being with me. She is happy and dancing now, but she told me if I ever need her, all I have to do is call for her and she will come to me. She isn't with me all the time. Just my Angel is with me all the time. Except he didn't come here with me and I don't know why not. He would like you, cause I like you." I gave her a hug. She got up and we walked hand and hand back to Daddy. When he saw us, he looked worried.

"Aunt Sadie, you haven't done anything to Debbe have you?"

"Yes, Earl, I have. Her wart will be gone in a couple of days and it will not come back."

I guess that made him feel better and he gave Aunt Sadie a hug.

"Thank you because that would be wrong to do that to a little child." We said good-bye and got in the car and went home. Angel was there when I walked in. He never answered me when I asked why he didn't come with me to Aunt Sadie's house.

Aunt Sadie made her transition home shortly after my visit. My wart went away and never came back. But I started to know things that people thought were wrong. I was called names, and when I started school, I was writing left handed. I was smacked with a ruler till I could write right handed. I didn't understand then, but as I got older and learned of the superstitions that people in Eastern Kentucky had and then I totally understood. Some of the tale, tale signs of being a witch were: red hair (mine started out red and ended up auburn), green eyes, being left handed and having the ability to know things, sometimes before they happened, sometimes as they were happening! Six out of six, that's pretty good. I haven't told anyone of my out of body experiences till I wrote this book. I am sure that was not allowed either.

Times have changed, if you have these gifts, use them, change the world for the better, grow understanding and love where you are, raise our worlds vibrations!

My Out of Body Experiences

When I was 6 years old, I lived in Corbin, Kentucky. It is the home of Colonel Sanders and Kentucky Fried Chicken. Then it was a very small town, with a small hospital. My Great Aunt Mary, cooked the meals at the hospital for the patients and on Sundays, the town folk would come and eat Sunday dinner there. I am sure the food wasn't healthy for the patients, but it was delicious comfort food.

I had a cold that I couldn't get rid of. Dr. Sanderland was working very hard trying to help me. There just weren't any medicines then that would kick it. One day, I couldn't really breathe and the breathing treatments with steam was making it worse for me. Mama called Dr. Sanderland and asked if he could see me that morning. My fever had sky rocketed and she couldn't get it down. He came to our house to see me. Then he used our phone. "I need an ambulance at 604 Walnut Drive. Yes to go to Lexington. Hurry." He seemed terribly upset. I could hear him talking to my mother rather roughly, but I was in and out of sleeping and couldn't really understand the conversations. I could her my mother saying "No, I swear she just got that 104 fever, it was down all night." The people from the ambulance came and Dr. Sanderland picked me up and carried me to the back of the ambulance. "Ok, Sparks, these people are going to take good care of you. They are taking you to Lexington to a big hospital there." "Are you going with me?" I squeaked out. "No, there will be no room. This is just your ride." I nodded my head and looked at my angel. He grinned. I knew I wasn't alone. The men came and stuck needles in my arm that really hurt. Then they pushed on my chest. I didn't feel really good. They put a mask over my mouth and nose. I was scared and held my breath. My angel looked at me and said "C----n, breathe. It will help you, I promise." He always called me C----n, at first I told him my name and my nickname but he would just smile, pat me on the head and say "Ok, C----n, but this is my name for you because we are best friends. Don't tell anyone this name."

We finally made it to the Lexington. I guess that was a town, at that time I didn't know. I woke up again in a really big bed. The nurses came in to put needles in my arms. They would pick up my arms; look at them, shake their heads and leave. They didn't look like any nurses I had seen at Corbin hospital when I went there. Those nurses were all dressed in white, including their legs and shoes. I could never figure out how their legs were so white. They also had on white caps with red stripes on them. These ladies were all dressed in black like my angel. I thought they were angels. Then there was a big commotion in the hallway, a really big angel came in and took my arm. She immediately with no trouble at all put the needle in my arm. It didn't hurt at all. She was talking to the other nurses when all of my machines started to make all kinds of noise.

The next thing I knew, Angel and I were in the corner of the room looking down. I looked so tiny! "Angel, am I really that small. I look tiny." "Yes, C----n, you are that tiny. That was part of the reason the Dr. couldn't help you." "Why are all of the machines making all that noise? Oh wow, I can breathe, listen no rattle. This is great! My chest doesn't hurt anymore." "Come, walk with me." We started walking down the hallway and I don't remember what we were talking about but it was a serious conversation. He was holding my hand as we walked. Then we turned the corner and I saw a long way away, a door. I knew it was a door because I could see light shining from it on three sides. I let go of his hand and ran as fast as I could go to the door. I grabbed the door knob and tried to open it. "C----n, you can't open it." I put my foot beside the door and pulled with all my might. "I want to go back; I don't like it here." "You can't go back it's not time. You have work to do or have you forgotten about that?" "I don't care about it anymore; I want to go home." I continued to pull on the door to no avail. I wasn't getting tired but I wasn't giving up either, I was determined to get through the door. Then we were back in the hospital room and all the machines were humming right along. I looked at Angel. "This isn't fair; you are not being nice to me. I don't want to be here." "You have no choice child." At that moment, I was in the bed, chest hurting and rattling. I could barely breathe. Too deep and I would cry. The big Angel was explaining to the other angels around her, "In order to hit the vein on an arm this tiny, you have to angle the needle and be very careful not to go through the vein, because it is tiny too. We almost lost her, keep an eye on this one. Her lungs collapsed on the way up here. It's a miracle she is alive. Let's keep her that way. They will be coming for her to take her back any minute." I had a hard time staying awake. When I woke up again, I was on a rolling bed going down the hallway. I sat up as we went through the big doors. Running down the hallway was my Daddy, yelling "I love you Sparks, I'll be here when you come out." Then I was asleep. I didn't know that Daddy was only called after the ambulance left on its way with me to Lexington. They told him I probably would not make the trip up there but it was the only chance I had. He left work and drove the three-hour trip alone. There was no interstate back then.

I never told anyone about being on the ceiling, for fear they would be angry with me about that too.

The only other time I had an out of body experience was in 1975 when I was pregnant with my first son, John David. I was a long term substitute teacher at Bowling Green Junior High School. I was teaching Art, in the Art room that I had in high school. It was very familiar and I loved the job. I was right in the middle of the class telling them how to break a picture down into squares to copy it. Then I was seeing my huge pregnant self, dressed in my blue dress with the red scarf around the v neck. I had no idea I was so huge! I watched me for a while teaching and thinking what a good job I was doing. As I walked around the room, the students were engaged and all of them were trying to grid off their papers. I was impressed with me. Then I was back in my body. I thought right then that I need different shoes with this dress!

My son is now 45 and I have not had another out of body experience. I have astral traveled. If you have ever jerked yourself awake during the night, you also have astral traveled, you just don't remember it. Check into it.

My First Vision

It was the summer of 1964. I had just turned 13!! I was living back in Corbin, Kentucky with my mother and my sister. My Dad was living in Cincinnati, Ohio. I was not happy about my parents splitting up, actually that isn't true. I wasn't happy about being with my mother instead of my Daddy. My mother and I fought a lot, I never realized why until I was much, much older and wiser. But here I was at 13 in Corbin. I loved being in the same town with my grandparents and getting to visit with them all the time certainly helped the transition.

I had finished seventh grade in Corbin, and was playing clarinet in the high school band. We were all getting ready to go to band camp! How cool was that?

One Friday evening in July, my mother and I had gotten into a really bad fight. I was leaving to go to band camp in two weeks and this needed to be settled.

"Mama, I think we need to put this argument behind us. I don't want to go to band camp upset with you or you upset with me."

"Ok honey, I am not upset. You just don't understand how the world works yet and I definitely know how it works."

"Well I can tell you that I know for certain that you are going to have to pick a life and stay there. You cannot live on both sides.

God will take you out. The car wreck you had last year was your warning shot."

"You don't know anything about that, you talk like you are grown. You're not. At least not yet."

"Don't you know how serious this really is?"

"Enough, we have settled it, now go practice."

I looked at angel, he knew that what I was saying was true. Life could get real serious really quickly. I went to my room at the back of the house. I had no trouble falling to sleep. I woke up sometime before dawn, screaming and crying. Although I was afraid to break the silence, I was more afraid to be alone. "Mama!" I called several times before I woke her up. Her bedroom was on the opposite side of the house. I could hear her coming across the house slowly. I am sure she was upset I woke her up but I was still crying and I didn't care at that time what punishment was coming. When she got to my doorway, she could hear me sobbing. She didn't turn on the light. The moon was full and shining in. She rushed to the bed and sat down beside me, holding and patting me on the back.

"It's just a bad dream honey. That's all, just a bad dream."

"No, it isn't. It's what is going to happen to you if you don't change."

"That's silly, how could you possibly know the future?"

"The Whisperers told me what to say to you earlier, and you didn't listen to me. They showed me tonight. You are going to die in a car wreck. A lot like the one on Glasgow road last year. You will not have on your seatbelt and the car flips and you are thrown out and it lands on you. You are killed instantly. It happens on the Falls Road. I promise it is going to happen to you if you don't change."

She looked at me seriously. "You saw that? You saw it happen?"

"Yes, I saw it happen and Sherry and I are here at the house.

I look at the clock it's 10:30, Granddaddy calls and tell me that you were in a car wreck and that you are at the hospital. He comes to take us to the hospital, but when he comes in, he says "Girls, your mother was killed tonight in a car wreck. I'm taking you to

Wilma's house." I run out the door and try to head across the street. He catches me and drags me back, kicking and screaming to his car. Sherry doesn't seem the least bit upset. We ride to Wilma's house and she gives us both big hugs and puts us to bed in the front bedroom. Sherry is sound asleep and I am awake listening to them talk. They call Daddy to come get us. Oh Mama, please change. Quit your jobs at the church or quit the other. I don't care which one but you cannot do both. You just can't." I was sobbing again. She just hugged me. She didn't argue with me, tell me I was wrong, she just hugged me till I went back to sleep.

What I am going to tell you now I did not find out till years later. My mother went back to her room, picked up the phone and called my Daddy. "Earl, she's had a dream about me." "Do you know what time it is?" "Are you listening to me, Debbe has had a dream about me!" "Ok, what was it about?" "Me dying. She told me in great detail." "How would she know that?" "You know very well how she would know. It's exactly what we suspected. Your Aunt Sadie, passed it on to her instead of you." "Jean, you are getting hysterical, calm down. What do you think Aunt Sadie passed to her and when and how? That's impossible." "She was not called a witch because she baked cookies for the church bazaar, Earl." "When do you think she had a chance to do this?" "When you got that wart charmed off her thumb. That's when she offered it to you and you refused. That's when she gave it to Debbe." "You woke me up to discuss Aunt Sadie?" "NO, I woke you up to ask you when this happens, come and get the girls. I do not want my mother to raise them. Look what she did to me." "Ok sure, but nothing is going to happen to you. Go to bed and get some sleep." "Sure, you promise me? Say it!" "Yes, Jean, I will come and get the girls if something ever happens to you." "Ok, thank you. Good night." "Nite" The following Monday morning Mama went to the family attorney to get her will drawn up. She was to come back in two weeks and sign the papers. The attorney told her it was a strange request since she was only 38 and in good health. She came back in two weeks to sign the papers and was told that Hermann Like was not there, he had gone to a UT football game and that she would need to come in on Monday. She didn't live to see that Monday. This conversation was told to me by my Daddy many years later, when I asked him about it.

I had allergies and had to have allergy shots every week. Dr. Sanderland, taught my mother how to give me the shots, all she had to do was purchase the medicine. I am pretty sure that my Papa Kam purchased the meds for me.

Two weeks later, nothing had changed in my mother's life and I was getting anxious. I got a phone call from my friend Beverly. "Say, can you come spend the night with me tonight?" "Mama, Bev wants me to spend the night tonight is that ok?" "Just be home in time for your shot tomorrow. We have to finish packing your suitcase for band camp and make sure you have everything. You leave on Sunday." "Ok." "Hay, Bev, I'm headed your way." I spent the night and we stayed up listening to records and talking. We had a lot of planning to do since we were going to band camp on Sunday! We were so excited, sleep didn't come. We watched the sun rise, and then fell asleep.

The next morning, we slept in a lot later than I wanted to. I started walking home, which was a couple of miles, not far. When I got to 5th street, I saw my mother driving toward town. I yelled at her to stop. I was going to go with her. I have no idea if she heard me or not, but she didn't stop. I walked home. There was a note saying Sherry was at Wilma's house and that she had headed to town to get my allergy medicine. Ok, that didn't sound bad. Nowhere near the Falls road, so far so good. Sherry came home early afternoon and Mama still had not returned. I was starting to get concerned. I phoned the pharmacist to see if Mama had made it there. "Hello, this is Debbe Wilson, I was calling to see if my mother had come by there? I saw her this morning and she was driving to town to get my allergy medicine. Have you seen her?" "Sure Deb, she's fine. She got your meds and while she was in here, I got a call from La Follette Hospital to see if I had some medication they were out of, I told them I did but I had no way to get it to them. When I told your mother the story she immediately volunteered to take the medicine down there. The man injured in the explosion was a friend of the family. She collected the medicine and the address of where and to whom she would deliver it to, she left to go down there. That's been a bit ago, I am sure she is ok. She probably just stayed to visit for a bit. Don't worry, she will be fine."

I hung up knowing that she would not be fine. I found out years later that she delivered the medicine and then headed to Rogers Dock to have a beer with friends before she headed back home. On the way back to Corbin, it started to rain and she lost control of the car in a curve. The car flipped and threw her out of it, with the car landing on top of her. Killing her instantly.

Meanwhile, my sister and myself were home, waiting for Mama to arrive. I wanted to make sure everything was ready for my trip to band camp and that I had not forgotten anything. I called Bev, we went over the list and checked them off. We were set!

Sherry and I started making supper, it was getting late. If Mama had not eaten there would be something for her to eat. We had supper, did the dishes. I started to panic. Then we sat down on the couch, I looked at the clock, 10 o'clock!! NO!! I was screaming in my head. I looked at my sister and started crying. "Mama's dead. Granddaddy will call in just a minute and tell us she was in a car wreck and that she's fine in the hospital. Then he will get here at 10:30 and take us to Wilma's house. Daddy will come in the middle of the night and get us. We will go live with him. "Stop lying! You are scaring me!" Then the phone rang. I answered it, I didn't say hello, I just listened to the information I was given two weeks earlier. I sat back on the couch with my sister. I was still crying. "Well who was that? What did they say?" "I already told you who it was and what they said." She looked at me like I was a freak. The doorbell rang and Granddaddy was standing there. "Girls your mother was killed in a car wreck tonight. I'm here to take you to Wilma's house." I ran past him and out the door. He finally caught me before I could get across the street. He took us to Wilma's house. She put us in the front bedroom and went to call my Daddy. I was awakened by him early in the wee hours of the morning. He had driven straight through from Cincinnati! After the funeral, we went back to Bowling Green to live with our Daddy.

That was my first vision, but not by far my last one. Don't be afraid of what you know or see. It is all part of a miraculous plan. Even when it looks like it's as bad as it can get. It is still part of the plan.

Granddaddy

My Granddaddy was Robert L Smith. He was a major player in my life. He and I were very close. He owned and operated IGA grocery in Corbin, Kentucky. He had fought in two wars and had seen a great deal in his life. He was the only pleasure I had going to my Dad's parents' house. I had heard all kinds of stories from him, tips on fishing, and how to live life.

He was the one who taught me to cuss and smoke! Yep right in his basement when I was in grade school. As soon as I tried out my new words on my Mother, I thought she was going to stroke out!

"Who taught you to say such filth!"

"Nobody." I knew we were in huge trouble, because I had never seen her so crazy mad. When the truth finally came out and it wasn't from me. He found out the punishment I was enduring; he went to see my Mother.

"Jean, stop this crazy punishment, Debbe didn't know what I was teaching her was wrong. I thought it was cute."

"It isn't cute; how could you possibly think that was right? Where is your moral compass?" I wasn't sure what a moral compass was, but if anybody had one it was Granddaddy, I loved him so. What is so wrong with shit? It's another word for poop and easier to say.

"Well let me tell you BOB, if she learns anything else from you, she will not be allowed to come and visit you, ever! Do you understand me?"

"Yes, I will not teach her anything else." What?! How can I learn about life if he doesn't teach it to me. Wow! Maybe I just need to avoid showing what all I learn, maybe that's the answer. I can't imagine not going to the store and playing in the back.

After that we just kept things to ourselves. Mother never learned that I had been taught to smoke. When we moved from Corbin when I was in the 3rd grade, I would go home on weekends and Granddaddy and I went fishing a lot. Just sitting on the water talking. He was always interested in what I was doing in school. It started out they thought that maybe he could make me less unhappy about being in Lexington, Kentucky. Nope I hated that place, the people were mean and I didn't fit in. Then I got sent to a new school downtown and Granddaddy came to Lexington to see me. We went to get ice cream. "Sparks, you need to start talking to your Dad and not take matters into your own hands." "Why?" "Because your hands are little and his hands are big. He can fix things the right way because he knows how to do that and right now you are not old enough to know how to do that. OK? Or if your Dad is out of town you can call me collect. We can talk about it. Does that work?"

"Ok. I'll talk to one of you if things get bad again, promise. But, I can't let anyone make my sister cry! It's not right."

"That's true, it's not right, and we can fix it for you so it doesn't happen again."

"You think he will make someone else cry?"

"No, I don't, I think what you did will stay with him his whole life. But, as a young lady, you can't do that anymore. Young ladies don't act like that."

"I did warn him that he should stop and I did tell him what I was going to do. It wasn't a surprise."

"It was a surprise to a lot of people, me included. But what's done is done and we are not going to act like that anymore, right?"

"Right."

That was the kind of relationship I had with my Granddaddy.

Fast forward to Sunday, May 15th 1966. I was having a dream about my Granddaddy. He looked so young!

"Sparks, I want you to know that I love you and that I will always be with you. You need anything just call my name and I will help you."

"Why are we having this conversation? I call you once a week and we talk; what's really up?"

"You are not going to be able to do that anymore honey."

"Why?"

"Because I am going away physically, but I will be with you Spiritually. I know you understand, because you knew when you mother had left."

"I knew that because I dreamed it two weeks before and I tried to help her change and stay but she didn't want to. She was tired."

"I am tired too baby. No, don't cry. I will be ok, I am ok, promise."

I woke up crying and my foot feeling very hot. I looked down and my electric blanket was smoking. I threw it off the bed and unplugged it. I sat on my bed, crying.

"DADDY! DADDY!" My Dad came running down the hallway.

"What's wrong?" He sat down on the side of my bed.

"Granddaddy is dead."

"Sparkie, Granddaddy isn't even sick. You have had a bad dream."

"Yes, I did have one, but he is dead. Call Grandmother and see if I am not right. I'm telling you he is dead."

"It's 5 o'clock in the morning, your Grandmother isn't even up yet."

"Of course she is. She is at the kitchen table reading her Bible. She starts at 4."

"Ok, I will call. You sit here I'll be back. I know you are wrong."

I had not stopped crying. I knew I was right but I just needed proof. My mother died in a car wreck in 1964. I had dreamed about how it was going to be for me and my sister. We were alone at the house and Granddaddy called then came out to the house to get us. That's what I dreamed and that's what happened. If you want more details, read My First Vision. I didn't have any conversations with her after she passed that I remember. I had never really had any conversations with people who have passed, so this being a first, I wanted to make sure it was real and that it could happen again.

Daddy came back into my room.

"Grandmother didn't answer the phone, which is odd. Even if she is asleep, she would get up and answer the phone, I let it ring a long time.

"Daddy, call the hospital; ask for Bob Smiths' room."

He didn't say anything he just looked at me oddly and walked back to his bedroom where there was a phone. I heard him talking but I couldn't understand what was being said. In a bit, he walked back into my room and just looked at me with tears running down his cheeks and shook his head yes. I jumped up and ran to him, we stood there in a hug for a long time, both of us crying, saying nothing.

"How did you know?"

"He came to me in my dream and told me. He looked so young."

"He had gone to the doctor on Friday, with abdominal pain. The doctor told him it was gas and sent him home. It got worse Saturday night and his appendices ruptured at 3 this morning. They took him to the hospital in an ambulance. He had emergency surgery at 4 but it was all over his abdomen by then. They couldn't clean it up and his heart failed at 4:45 this morning. Oh honey, I am so sorry."

"I guess I was the first one he came to. Geeze." We both stood there crying.

Later that day we drove the 3.5 hours to Corbin to support and help my Grandmother. On the trip over we told stories about the man he was and how much we will miss and love him.

When you lose someone close to you, just remember the person they were and why you loved them so very much. Telling funny or touching stories about them will ease your soul and release them to the next phase of their journey.

A Secret Passage

I graduated high school in 1969, from Bowling Green High School. As a graduation present, my Daddy gave me a trip to Europe with my high school art teacher, Betty Anderson. Our Art Club was taking the trip and we were going to study comparative government. I had the best time of my life. The group from my home town connected with other groups from around the USA and we traveled in busses and trains all over Europe.

We came over from New York on a ship named the Rotterdam. It was the first time I had ever been on the ocean. I was in love. I loved the smell, the sights, the water, I loved it all! On the way over, I was in the bathtub and all of a sudden, I was out of the tub and under the sink! I got up, dried off and slipped into some clothes and stumbled out of the doorway into the hall. I was being thrown from side to side. On the way down the hallway, I saw another person. "What is going on?" "We have hit a storm and everyone is supposed to be in their cabins." That was good to know. "Why are you out of your cabin then?" "I'm sick." Then she threw up on me. Well ok, yes you are. I went to my cabin and changed clothes quickly. "Laura, we are in a storm are you ok?" "No, I feel awful." "Well I'm heading to find something to eat." "Shut up! The thought of it is making me sick!" I left and took my chances going down the hallway. Whew, no people and the hallway had been cleaned. Wow that was fast. I made my way to the deck to look for the grill master whose name was John. I went out on deck and saw the ocean was in an angry fit throwing mood! Waves were taller than the ship and wind and rain was coming down in torrents. Before I could venture to the railing, my arm was grabbed. "What the hell are you doing out here. You all are supposed to be in your cabins!" "Well I was in the tub and found myself under the sink. So I got dressed and came up here. I was looking for John." "John's not out here, now get inside." "Yeah, I see that. Where is he, I'm hungry." "Your what?" "I'm hungry." "Are you kidding me?" "No, I would like something to eat, I'm not real particular. But I'm hungry." "Come with me we are going to see the captain." "Oh wow that would be cool, does he have food?" We made out way to the helm where the captain was doing battle with the ocean. The guy who caught me on the deck, told the captain and then said, "She's hungry. Do you believe that shit?" The captain looked at me and started to laugh. "I have never been on a boat like this before. Wow you can see everything from up here." "That's because this is NOT a boat, she's a ship." "Oh, sorry. I have never been on a SHIP before. I have a question, where can I get something to eat. I'm really hungry." "Well the only place open for eating is for sailors in the galley. Do you mind eating with them? It's not fancy food." "Good, and no I don't mind. Thank you." "Take this young lady to the galley, please. Hay, what's your name?" "Debbe Wilson." "Pleased to meet you Miss. Wilson. Enjoy your dinner." We then went down to the galley. It was in the bowels of the ship. Oddly enough there was less movement there than topside. I walked in an all of the conversations stopped. I looked around at all of the people there who were staring at me like I didn't belong, and wondering what I was doing there. "Hello, my name is Debbe and the captain said I could come and get something to eat. I'm hungry." They all stared at me like I was crazy then one man stood up and stretched out his arms, "Welcome Debbe, to our humble abode. I assume you are a sailor?" "Ummm, no. I've never been on the ocean or on a boat, sorry, ship like this before. Can I still stay?" "Wait this is all new to you and you're not seasick?" "Well no but several of the others are, I have been thrown up on, does that count?" "Man she was in the tub and got thrown." before he could finish everyone said "Under the sink!" and everyone laughed. "Well Mother Ocean has initiated you into the family. Welcome!" I ate and talked and had a fantastic time. It was getting late and we had a curfew. "Thank you all for such a great time, but I have a curfew and need to get back to my room. I had a great time." As I made my way to my cabin I saw several people in the hallways. I knew better than to slow them down, I just got out of their way. I slept like a baby on the top bunk.

The next day was a repeat of the last. I found no one that was up for eating. I ate in the galley with the crew. The ship was tossed so much that you could stand on the steps and if you timed it right, you could step to the next landing! It was great fun. I visited with the Captain a good deal. "This is the worst storm I have seen in all of my 30 years on the ocean. Tomorrow promises to be beautiful. If you're up early, you will be able to see some sea turtles." "Oh, I will definitely get up for that. Around sun rise?" "That's the time." "We will be coming into the White Cliffs of Dover day after tomorrow. That's quite a site as well. Look for the Dolphins port side." "Which side is port side?" "Remember it this way, port has 4 letters and left has 4 letters." "Got it." I learned a lot from that man in the 9 days it took to cross the Atlantic. The trip was supposed to be a quick 7 days. I saw my first sea turtle, dolphin, seagull, and whale. It was a wonderful time.

While in Piccadilly Circus, I met a US solider. When the group went to see the Crown Jewels, he and I went driving through the country side. We stopped to see a castle that was on no tourist map. It was huge and not very well kept, but I felt connected to it, so I talked him into taking a tour through it. Half way through the tour, we were at the bottom of a stone staircase that wound around stone walls, that were cold and unforgiving. As I stood there looking at them, I saw a passageway behind them in my mind. "Why don't we take the secret passage?" The lady, who was dressed in a very plain cotton printed dress, stopped and looked at me. Not shocked but, with wonderment on her face. She smiled, "Child there isn't a secret passage. There are always rumors of secret passages but not every castle has them. I have given this tour for years and I clean this castle. Trust me if there was one we would take it." I smiled back at her knowing I was right, not questioning why I knew that only that I knew. "Well, what do you call that?" And I hit a stone under a torch, and part of the wall moved. It creaked, at first I thought I had actually broken something. How did I know that was there? The passage was dark and dusty; cob webs were hanging down. I knew I had been there before. I knew immediately that I was in trouble. The kind woman was now screeching "What have you done? You have damaged the castle! We will have you arrested! HELP! Guards!" The kind woman was very distraught now. I looked around for the solider, he was gone. There I stood. "I can close it." "Don't you dare touch anything else." The guards came, when they saw the passage they called someone to come to the castle. I sat down on the bottom step. Good thing we were the only ones there. After a while a very nicely dressed man came. "Come with me. Humm we have wondered about that for years." I followed him to an office. The bobbies were there, very sharply dressed. He dismissed them. I took a seat and gave a sigh of relief. At least I wasn't going to be arrested, that was good news. "I have a few questions for you, Miss Wilson." He was looking at my passport. I had to give them my identification before I could go through the castle. "Yes, sir. I can shut it if you'd like." "Yes, I'm sure you can. What I don't understand is how did you know it was there?" "I can't tell you that." "Oh I am afraid you are going to have to tell me precisely that." "Oh sorry, I didn't mean I would not tell you if I knew but that I really don't have a clue how I knew that was there." The interrogation went on with questions like, where was I really from, what was I really doing in England, why did I stop at their castle. After an hour, I was asked if there was anything else I could show them. I really thought they should have started with that one, but what do I know. "I assure you, I am not a spy nor do I hold any ill will toward you or your castle. I have no idea how I knew that was there and I am very sorry that I did that and I will not do anything like that again." "You can leave but please do not come back to our castle." "I didn't get to finish the tour I paid for." "No, you didn't and no you do not get a refund." "Hum, my ride left me and I have no way back to London except for walking, which I do not mind to do if you can point me in the correct direction, please." I was given my passport back and a lift by the nicely dressed man, who I later found out was a detective, in London.

I did check the papers while I was in London to see if there was a castle that discovered a new passage way. But nothing was reported. The rest of the time in Europe was didn't compare to that day in England.

My Russian Friend

In the 1970's, I had been introduced to the Slavic Gospel Association. This was an organization that had decided to help the persecuted Christian worshipers of Russia, the former USSR, through prayer. I'm not sure how I found out about this organization, but I knew I could be a prayer warrior for them. I received rectangular cards from the organization. These cards had the person's picture on them, their names, what they were caught doing, what prison they were being held in or if the person was just missing. It also contained their birth dates and arrest or missing dates. These people, both men and women, who were being persecuted in Russia for their religious beliefs became very real to me. I prayed for them daily for about two years. Then the strangest thing happened.

I was substitute teaching in sixth grade for a small, mostly black elementary school. My class was coming back from lunch, when I heard one of the boys start fussing at another boy. "Commie, you're no good." "Go back home, you don't belong here." I walked back to where the boys were.

"Ok, what is the problem?"

"He's a Commie." Replied the student., pointing to a very unhappy, poorly dressed boy. I looked at the boy, his clothes were ill fitting, his black straight hair needed a trim, and his striking blue eyes had tears in them.

"Come here honey." I said as I put my arm around him. I could tell his eyes had seen a lot for one so young. I sent the class into the room with work to do, and leaving the door open so I could hear them working.

"So, is it true that you are from Russia?" He said nothing, looking like he wanted to die.

"You know it is ok that you are from Russia. I pray for people from Russia every day."

"Really? How do you know Russians? You go there?"

"No, but I can show you the people that I pray for. They are on cards I have the cards in my car. Maybe you can see them after school?" He looked at me like he didn't believe me.

"Now let's go into the class and help them to understand that you are not their enemy. OK?" He buried his face into me, hugging me and started to cry.

"It's going to be just fine, I promise." I patted his head. It had taken a lot for him to break down. He looked up wiped his eyes and nodded. We walked into the classroom. It was filled with students that had seen a lot as well. I started a discussion about persecution and how and why people are persecuted. What we thought persecution was and why was persecution wrong for anybody. Then we talked about how we as people could stop it. How one person at a time could stop persecution. Then the main question was presented.

"Did you know that calling Vladimir a "Comie", is a very easy way to persecute him?"

"Making him feel different, just because he was born in Russia, is that wrong?"

"Do we get to choose where we are born? What we look like? Who our parents are? What our names are?"

I waited for the class to answer. Then came the resounding "NO"

"Then should we hold out our hands in friendship to people who come to America for a better life?" Several heads were nodding.

"These people could have picked anywhere in the world they wanted to go and they chose our country! Why? Because we love to help people who want to do better, who want to live better, who want to worship the way they choose, and who want to become a part of our family."

"Now I want you all to make Vladimir feel welcome. He can tell you all about a place you may never get to visit. I have never been there. It's a beautiful country, with beautiful people. Some of these people cannot worship the way they want to."

"How would you feel if on Sunday, when you were in church, the police came in and took your preacher away? Then they made everybody leave and they put a lock on the door, so you could not come back. That is what is happening right now in Russia. Vladimir and his family came here so they could worship the way they wanted to. Please make him feel wanted."

At the end of my speech, Vladimir was looking at me like I had three heads. I could see he was wondering how I knew all of that information about him. That didn't last to long because the students all got out of their seats and gathered around to welcome him into their class. They exchanged stories about food, and clothing, and what they did to have fun. I counted it as world history and left the teacher a note about it.

"School is over Vladimir; can I give you a ride home?" We had stopped at the office to see what bus he would be taking in the morning and what time it came. I wanted to make sure his mother and family knew he would have transportation to and from school.

When we got to his house, he got out of the car and his mother came running out of the house. "Is he in trouble? Did he do something wrong? Was he fighting again?" It seems he had been in several fights since they arrived two weeks before. I shared what happened at school and that I thought all of the fighting would be over with now. She was very pleasant. Then I told her about the Slavic Gospel Association, she nodded, but said nothing.

"Russia is a huge country Miss."

"Yes, I know Russia is a huge place and that the odds of you knowing any of the people I have been praying for is slim to none. If the situation were reversed I would tell you not to hold out a whole lot of faith in me knowing anyone, but would you be up for just looking and see?"

She laughed, "Ok, but don't expect too much."

I went back to the car and got the cards out of my bag. I had them with me to show a friend after school. I came back with the cards and she invited me into her home and gave me a glass of tea. The kitchen was clean and smelled of fresh baked bread. The table was white and reminded me of my Grandmother's kitchen table. There was a warm loving spirit in this house.

I handed the stack of 25 cards to her and said, "I know the chances are slim, and I appreciate you taking time…" I stopped talking when I heard her gasp and start sobbing. Tears were streaming down her face. She looked up. "Where did you get these?!!"

"I asked the Slavic Gospel Association for names of people I could pray for who are being persecuted for their religious beliefs. They sent me these people to pray for and I have for two years. Why are you crying?"

She came over to me still crying and hugged me. When she finally calmed down, she told me why she was crying.

Still holding the cards, she showed me one card after another saying,

"This is my father. He escaped and is here with me now."

"This is my grandmother. She died in that prison."

"This is my preacher. Vladimir was the one he was illegally baptizing when they caught him and took him away. Vladimir was so young they let him go."

"This is my uncle. I didn't know he was captured."

And on and on it went till she came to the last card. That's when she started to wail.

"This is my brother. I didn't know he had been captured."

She had either been related to or known everyone I had been

praying for, over the last two years. Some she didn't know about, others she filled me in on.

Later, I contacted the Association to give them an update on the people who had passed or escaped and so they could be encouraged that their work had a profound effect on the lives of the people that they found prayer warriors for.

Just imagine, I had been praying for people I didn't know in Russia and they were led to my hometown in Kentucky!

I left her house and went to my pastor's office. I told him the story. He wanted to meet her. I took him with me back to her house. It was in a very bad section of town and was too small for a family of five, but it was what they could afford. My pastor helped them to move into a larger house in a better part of town. He also helped Vladimir's parents to get better jobs. We as Americans, do love to help people stand on their own two feet.

I am sure when you are on your illuminated path, that you are helping people. Always, your seemingly insignificant actions are connected to a huge picture that you cannot see. Just know it's there and everything you do effects the outcome. Make your choices wisely and listen to your WHISPERERS!

Controlling My Anger

Wayyy back in the mid 1990's, before I admitted who I was really, and what I was supposed to be doing, I was shown part of me, that I didn't know I had. I came to the realization that I had more power at my control than I had ever thought about having.

I was dating a man that invited me to go to Florida with him and stay at his parent's home in Panama City. I accepted the offer. We had been exclusively dating for a while now and I thought we were getting serious. At least I was serious. It was February, right after Valentine's Day. I had gotten 12 long stemmed red roses, delivered to me at work. I was as impressed as the entire office was. Life was good!

We were packed up and headed to Florida! How great is that??

"It was so great of you to send me those roses at work! It really made me feel special! Thank you again. I was the envy of the office." I went on for a few minutes, he was smiling and I thought it was because of what I was saying. This is where in a text you would insert LOL.

"I am glad you liked them. Lisa doesn't like roses, so I sent her a plant. I hope she likes it too." "WAIT!! WHAT!! (Yes, I was shouting.) You sent Lisa (his old girlfriend) a plant?"

"Yes, because she doesn't like roses and it was Valentine's Day."

"What the FUCK! You have to be kidding me!"

"Why are you upset? I always send her flowers and plants on holidays. But this year I saved the roses for you. I sent her a plant."

It's probably a good thing I was now so angry I was speechless! What does one say to that?? Damn I was dumb? I sat there quiet. He didn't know me well enough to know that if I get really quiet – that's not a really good sign. LOL!! The anger started building inside of me. Instead of verbally fighting with him, that was obviously pointless, I did something I had never done before, I started internalizing the anger. It kept growing, and growing, and growing. We were already in Florida, so there was no way out of this horror show. If I had been a cartoon character, my head would have exploded and steam would be rising! I started staring at the floor, then the right corner of the floor, right above the tire. You know the type of mental conversation I was having with myself, we all know. We have all been there, well maybe not right there in the car trapped, but you get the picture. The longer I sat there the madder I became! All of a sudden he was screaming at me. What? We were pulling off the interstate to the side of the road.

"Didn't you hear anything I was saying?"

"Why, No I stopped listening to you a while ago." I didn't look at him, I didn't ask what was wrong, I personally felt like I could beat it no matter what it was.

He was shouting again. Wait what was he saying?

"We just had a blowout! I can't believe it! These are brand new tires, I bought them for this trip!"

Then it registered, I had mentally concentrated all of my anger in the direction of the tire on my side of the car!! WOW! He was talking again.

"Get out we need to go get help."

"No, you get out, you go get help. I'll be right here, no worries. I will wait with the car."

"It's hot, you need to come with me."

"You need to get out of my face, I am not going. You're a big boy hike up that highway."

'Well I don't know where to go." I didn't touch that one. My lips were sealed. So he got out of the car. I rolled down the windows and pulled out a book, to look comfortable.

After he left, I got out to look at the tire. Did I really do that?? The tire was not just blown; it was off the rim! When he got back with the mechanic, I was calmed down sort of. The mechanic got out and looked at the tire. I could tell by his face he was confused.

"You said this was a blowout."

"Yes, you can see by the tire that it is blown, right?"

"NO, this tire exploded from the inside out. I have never ever seen any tire do that. The tire isn't hurt, it has no cut, no hole. It's like it was filled with too much air and exploded off the wheel. That's the only way this could have happened."

He changed the tire came up to Brian with the paperwork for him to sign.

"Say what are you going to do with that tire and wheel?"

"I have no use for either of them."

"Would you care if I kept it? I really have never seen anything like it. I'd like to show it to some other folks to see if they have ever seen anything like this."

"Have at it." Brian looked at me, "So, are you ready to go? We are almost there."

I didn't answer I just got in the car. I didn't have the heart to tell him if he wanted another spare he would need to have that wheel to put it on. But then maybe that's about the price of a plant.

When we started down the highway, I knew for sure that I had accidentally sent all of my anger to that tire. After that, I kept a better handle on my anger and in what direction I send it.

Isaac and Sarah Elizabeth Messer

My great-grandfather was Isaac Messer. He was tall man over 6 foot and from German descent. I am told that he had thick silver hair he wore in a flat top. He perished from heat stroke. He was in the field cutting the hay with a sickle in 102-degree heat. He was in his 90's when he died. His wife was known as Big Mammie and he was known as Big Pap. Isaac Messer was a very strict and determined man. He saw Big Mammie when she was young and decided he wanted to marry her. His wife had died and left him with 3 children to raise. He asked Big Mammie's Dad for her hand in marriage. He refused him. He wanted his daughter to marry for the first time to someone who didn't already have a family. Much later that night, Isaac put a ladder up to Big Mammie's room on the second floor of her house and took her with him. He had a preacher at his house and the preacher married them that night. He was very protective of his family.

The next morning when she didn't come down for breakfast, her Dad went to her room, she was not there and he started cursing Isaac Messer. He got on his horse and rode over to Isaac's farm. Isaac was waiting for him, shotgun in hand. He told him that they were married last night and he would kill him if he came any further into his property. Big Mammie's Dad left.

The families did make amends and were together for all holidays and birthdays. This was eastern Ky., and that was the way Isaac Messer was. My grandmother told me this story about her parents. Isaac died long before I was born. I do remember Big Mammie however. She was a very tall woman around 6 foot and she had large hands. I can remember trying to put my little hand around her pinkie finger and not being able to do it. She would laugh at me, a sweet lovely laugh. My grandmother also related to me that Big Mammie was about the age of his children and they all played together. Big Mammie had my grandmother and she had my father.

When my daughter, Sarah was born, she had been brought to me at 10:00 at night to nurse one last time. They forgot to come and get her. I just pilled the pillows around her so she wouldn't fall out of the hospital bed and we visited all night long. The Whisperers told me her name was Sarah. I started calling her Sarah all night long, my precious little girl! My husband and I had already decided on her name, which was Elizabeth Jean. Elizabeth for his sister Judy and Jean for my mother. It was decided long before we got here.

In the morning, the head nurse came in my room.

"Debbe, what are you doing with your baby?"

"Shuuu, she's sleeping. She just had breakfast."

"When did you get her? The babies are not out yet"

"I have had her all night. She's fine, I put pillows around us so she would be safe."

I thought her head was going to explode. She turned on her heels and practically ran out of my room. Another nurse came in and took Sarah with her. She didn't look too happy either. I personally thought I had taken great care of my daughter. I later found out that the nurse who was supposed to come and get her, had forgotten about her. She was fired.

Later that morning, the woman in charge of sending the names of the babies to Frankfort, KY., vital statics came in. She was very businesslike from the beginning. "What do you want your daughter's name to be?"

"Elizabeth Jean"

"Ok, thank you." She turned around to leave the room.

The Whisperers were not whispering now practically shouting. "Her name is Sarah!"

"Oh, please wait. Can I change that name?"

The woman was at the door already. She turned on her heels and walked unhappily back to my bed.

"Ok...... change it to what?"

"Sarah Jean......no, Sarah Elizabeth.......no, Sarah Elizabeth-Jean with Elizabeth-Jean hyphenated.

Each time I had started a name she had started a new card. She was so frustrated I thought she might explode and finally she said,

"I personally don't give a shit what you name her, are you sure that's the name because I am not changing it again."

"I'm sorry, yes I am sure she is Sarah Elizabeth-Jean with the middle name hyphenated. Thank you for being so patient." She just glared at me. Then I said "UM, Sarah is spelled S A R A H."

She looked at me one last time, like she could kill me pulled out another card, started writing on it and left. Then I was wondering how I could tell her Dad that her name was Sarah not the Elizabeth Jean we had agreed on?

We went home from the hospital and things were great! Pat at first didn't want a girl, he was ready for another boy. But he grew to love her dearly, took a whole day of her smiling at him to crush his heart, and wrap it around her little finger.

Fast forward several years. My grandmother had a fall and was going from the hospital to a nursing home in Bowling Green, KY. Daddy and I both lived in Bowling Green, just across town from one another and we visited often. He told me he was sending her to the nursing home near me because, he needed help taking care of her.

I had gone with him to Corbin to help clean out grandmother's house. I was in the hallway that divided the house from the bedrooms and the dining room. There was a table there that had a drawer in it. I opened the drawer and found a funeral register in it. I took it out, on the front was written Big Mammie in black magic marker. Oh, good, maybe I can find out what her name was. I opened the book and nearly fell over. Sarah Elizabeth Messer aka Big Mammie. OMS!!! She was named for Big Mammie and I never knew it. Isaac Messer loved his wife with all his heart. They had 14 children together! Her name was the last thing he said "Sarah Elizabeth, I have always loved you and I will always love you. I will protect you where I am going just like I have protected you in this life. I love you." When she was dying years later, she looked up and said "Yes, Big Pap, I am ready to come with you again." And she was gone, so the stories go.

Family stories are a key to your past as they have been mine. I believe Isaac Messer was the one who named my daughter Sarah. I believe this because when she was in grade school, she started seeing a man who was really tall and wore overalls, she doesn't remember ever seeing his face, but his overalls had one side unhooked. Isaac Messer, owned and worked on his farm. He was rarely seen in a suit; he was always in his overalls with one side unhooked. He was buried in his overalls with the typical one side unhooked.

Isaac stayed with Sarah at our house in Plano, KY. When we lived there, he would occasionally make himself known to all of us by taking pictures off the wall, closing doors, making loud footfalls and but would he show himself to Sarah. When she started telling me about the man she would see and talk to I didn't connect the dots. I was trying to find out who it could be when finally, I asked her what he looked like. She described the Isaac Messer I had heard about all my life! Shortly after that I found Big Mammie's funeral register. It made perfect sense to me.

When I was fixing the property up to sell, he made himself know on several occasions. One afternoon, I had finished painting and was cleaning my brushes in the garage. I heard NPR Morning addition coming from the bathroom. It was not morning, it was late afternoon and I thought I had unplugged the radio. I walked into the house and down the hall to the bathroom. The radio was unplugged, but NPR was on as loud as if the radio was plugged in and it was morning!

"Ok, Isaac, stop it! We are moving and I am selling this house."

"I don't want you to sell it and move."

"Well, I am sorry but I am selling it, get used to it."

Then NPR went off. I picked up the radio and set it by the front door. I walked through the house back to the garage. All of the paint in the cans was all over the floor. I just looked at the mess. I knew he was throwing one last fit. I had no idea how I was going to clean the concrete, or explain how it happened. Then I decided to talk to Isaac again.

"Isaac, you need to clean this up. It will not stop me from selling the house. I am not going to say we have a resident ghost because I know you will follow Sarah wherever she goes. So please clean this up."

I walked out of the garage and started loading things into the car. When I was finished, I walked back into the garage and picked up the paint cans that were now about half full, looked at the spotless floor and left saying thank you to a man that I never met, but came to love any way.

Does it surprise me that when I was "done wrong" by Cappy, that the hurricane that came through the marina that he and our boat was, had the name Isaac? No, it does not. He has been in my life for a very long, long time and I suppose he will remain close to me, righting wrongs and setting things right or imposing judgment on the aggressors.

Believe me, you have protectors as well. Everyone has Family Spirits that follow them around. Some interfere and some do not. They can only talk to you if you are listening, well that's not entirely true. They talk regardless if you are listening or not. It is not too late for you to start listening to them. If you are not meditating, that is a great way to start. Google it. Good listening!

Seeing and Talking to a Demon

I moved to Palm Beach, Florida in 1995. I bought a condo on A1A, right across the street from the Four Seasons Hotel. It proved to be a very enlightening move on so many different fronts. One summer day, it was a very pleasant temperature, so I walked over the bridge to Lake Worth. A quaint little town, with lots of shops containing all kinds of artwork, ice cream shops, clothing shops, metaphysical shops, it was a wonderful place to walk through. A beautiful little town. All the locals know each other. It was so friendly, I loved to visit there. I could smell the jasmine in the air. When I got to the business district, I saw an acquaintance. She was a friend of a friend; I had met her once or twice. She had a New Age gift shop. "Sparkie, come on into my shop and have a look around. You haven't been in here before have you?" "Nope, sure haven't." As I started through the door, the hairs on the back of my neck stood up and I felt a chill. I stopped. It felt like all of a sudden the temperature dropped 20 degrees! "I can't go in there, sorry." "That's ok, I'll get chairs and we can sit in the sun and talk. You look cold." She brought out chairs and we sat on the sidewalk and started to visit.

We had been talking for a few minutes, catching up, chit chatting. She had just had a birthday and a lot of us had gone to the party. She was interested in Robert. I had just met him. I was new to the group of friends, so I had nothing I could tell her about him.

I looked down and I heard her ask "Who do you believe Jesus Christ is?"

When I looked up, it wasn't her, it was her voice, but what I saw was not that woman! A snake like head was there looking at me! He had taken the place of her head. I thought I was seeing things! Without saying a word, I leaned in close. He leaned in closer. I moved my head to the right, he moved his head to the left to mimic my movements. Then I moved my head to the left!

He said "Why do you look so surprised? You know who I am."

I couldn't say a word; I was totally flabbergasted! He asked the original question again.

"Who do you believe Jesus Christ is?" I noticed when he talked this time he was making a hissing sound. I told him I believed that Jesus Christ was the son of GD. He got very angry and started giving me grounds for what he was saying. He ended with:

"How could someone as intelligent as you believe that nonsense?"

Then I said

"GD being real doesn't depend on me believing it or you believing it. He always has been and always will be. Some of us are connected to Him and some of us are not connected to Him. He is the Almighty Power of the Universe. It doesn't matter what name you give Him."

He was gone a quickly as he had appeared.

My acquaintance looked at me

My GD, Sparkie, you look like you have seen a ghost, you're pale, are you alright? Need some water, have you got over heated?"

I stuttered "No, I am not alright. I am going home, talk to you later."

I got up on shaky legs and walked home, still trying to sort out in my mind what the hell had just happened. When I got to my condo, I grabbed my sketchbook and drew a picture of the demon I had just had a conversation with. I attached it to the only picture of her that I had, a birthday celebration for our mutual friend Barbara.

Although that happened over twenty years ago in 1996, I still can see that demon's face. I tried to see it in her after that happened, but I never saw him again and never talked to him again. I have often wondered why that happened and what I was supposed to learn from it.

Many years later on October 28th, 2011, the first episode of Grimm came on the TV. I sat shocked to see this. It only finalizes for me that I am not the only person who had seen this happen. Because how they change is exactly what I saw happen. People who can go from being normal to demonic. It's real, they are there and they are real. I've seen them!!

Sarah's Wreck

I was sitting in our RV at the dining room table talking to a friend of mine, it was a cool autumn evening in Arkansas. The husbands were outside enjoying their own conversations. At 11 o'clock p.m., my phone rang. When I answered I heard:

"Mama?" It was John David, my oldest son.

"Yes honey, what's wrong, you sound really stressed?"

"It's Sarah, she's been in a car wreck. She has broken her neck and her back in two places."

I couldn't breathe as tears were running down my cheeks, it was as if all of the air in the room was suddenly sucked out! When I could finally breathe, I was sobbing holding the phone. Rose went out and got Cappy, my husband. "Cappy get in here, something is wrong with Sparkie, she's hysterical!"

He came flying in.

"What's wrong? Who's on the phone?" I couldn't talk just kept shaking my head. Finally, I got out "It's John, Sarah's hurt."

Cappy took the phone, "John, what's wrong? I have never seen your mother like this. She can't stop crying and trying to breathe."

"Ok, where is she? What hospital? Can she move her fingers and toes?"

I heard myself saying "No, she broke her neck." I come from the

53

generation of people who grew up knowing a broken neck meant a hospital bed, traction and never moving again. I could not imagine my vibrant, lively daughter in this condition. I was already figuring out how to set up the spare room to accommodate my daughter, and how or who we could get to take care of her while I was teaching. I certainly was going to need that job. As I was going through all of this process, Cappy was calling the hospital in Tampa. Then I heard.

"Yes, I would like to be connected to the emergency room. My daughter was in a wreck and brought in with a broken neck and back. Her name is Sarah Skinner. Yes, it happened tonight. What's her condition?" "Yes, we understood that, can she move her fingers and toes?"

"Well her mother is hysterical."

"Yes, she would love to speak to her, is that possible?" "Yes ma'am."

Suddenly the phone was in my hand and I heard myself say "Bethie?"

"Oh GOD, I told John not to call you. I'm fine Mama, really, I'm just fine!"

"I'm sure you are except that your neck and back are broken. I was calling to tell you I will be there tomorrow."

"Well, I'm fine. I don't want you to come down here."

"Good cause I did not call to ask permission; I was calling to let you know that I am heading your way tomorrow. I love you."

Then the phone went dead. I felt much better after talking to her and got out the map. I was hunting the best way to get to Tampa from Van Buren, Arkansas. My phone rang again.

"Hello"

"Mama, I was wondering if you and Cappy were going to Tampa?"

"Yes, John, I'm going Cappy just started this job, he is staying here. I plan on leaving at daylight."

"I'm looking at the map now to see the quickest way to get to Florida from here. Remember that hurricane just blew through

Mobile. I'll call Couse in the morning and find out about the road situation down there then." Couse was a dear friend and a sailing buddy who lived in Elberta, Alabama, not far from Mobile. He would know the driving situations.

"Ok, I am heading down there too. I call you when I leave Bowling Green in the am. My route will be easier and a straight shot. I love you. Try and get some sleep."

"You too baby, talk in the morning."

Being the oldest John felt someone should be with me, especially since I feel apart and no one has ever seen me do that. Well it was a surprise to me too. So here we were, John leaving from Kentucky and me from Arkansas.

I was up at 6 pacing around waiting for a decent hour to phone Couse. My husband had not been on the job two weeks yet and he was not due a paycheck for another two days! How was I going to get to Tampa and back? He told his boss what happened when he went into work that morning. His boss cut him a check early for me to be able to get down there and offered to purchase me a plane ticket. I was more than grateful for all of this kindness, but it put me leaving at 9 am. Slightly later then I had wanted to leave.

It was the 2004 hurricane season and the IVAN had just come through the gulf, and destroyed part of I-10 around Mobile, Alabama. I phoned Couse.

"You can't make it on I-10 through Mobile Sparkie, you will have to go around up in BFE Alabama. That's going to slow you down a lot. Do you have a map?"

"Of, course, Couse, I have a map. Ok, so I will plan on interstate till Mobile. Thank you so much."

"Be careful, I'll ride with you if you want."

"No, but ya know I love you for that. I'll be fine."

I was driving our Ford Ranger as quickly as I dare. A speeding ticket I didn't have time for. But the thought went through my head if I could convince the officer to go in front of me and we could really fly! Cappy and I had decided that I should take highway 19 when I hit the Florida line. When I crossed into Florida, it was early morning just past midnight. I had been talking to John while I was driving. Then there was heavy fog, and I was crying and praying. This was taking too long!! All of a sudden, out of the corner of my eye, I saw someone sitting in the passenger seat, riding with me!! I was so tired, not having slept at all the night before, and now I was scared!

I called John.

"UMMM guess what?"

"Ok what, you sound funny Mama, what's going on where are you?"

"I'm on 19, it's supposed to be quicker. Now I'm not so sure with all the heavy fog. But I was calling because, there is someone sitting in the passenger seat with me. I have my right hand up to block me seeing them."

"Wait, you have your right hand up blocking seeing them and you're holding the phone with your left hand? What hand is on the steering wheel? God Mother, put the phone down. Take hold of the steering wheel and talk to them. I'm hanging up now."

The phone went dead. Great. I put the phone down and took hold of the steering wheel.

"Ok, any other time, I would love to sit and visit with you, but I am having such a problem with almost loosing Sarah, that I really can't talk to you right now. Please forgive me. I just can't deal with visitors and this situation, I just can't do it."

I called John back. He was already at a motel resting on the outskirts of Tampa.

"Mama, there isn't anything with you, there is nothing there. It's your imagination. You're tired and things like that happen. Look over there, because I know you are still shielding your face. Is there anything there?"

"No, nothing is there. Thank you, I should be where you are in about twenty minutes. See you then." I hung up.

John had rented a motel room just outside of Tampa. He left

the room key on his back tire and he went to sleep. Visiting hours at the hospital didn't start till 8 and we thought we might be able to get some sleep. I finally got to the motel at 6:30 am, exhausted and relieved. It was still dark. I got the key and went upstairs to the room. After a hug hello and some discussion about whether we should go or not. "Look, it's been a long drive for you Mama, try and get some sleep. In about an hour we will head to the hospital." As I opened my bag to get out sleeping apparel, I immediately knew who had been riding with me. My entire bag smelled like my grandmother's cabin. She had passed several years before and always loved Sarah because she looked like my mother, who had passed in 1964. I pulled out a tee shirt and tossed it to John who had been watching me and wondered why I was crying again.

"Why does this smell like Mama Kam's cabin?"

"Because she was the one riding with me in the cab of the truck. I am so sorry I didn't figure it out then. I would have loved her company. She loved you guys a lot, but Sarah looked just like Mama, and she could never quite get over that fact. It makes sense that she would be along on this ride."

"Well yeah, they did look identical if the pictures are any indication."

"Ok, John I am not going to be sleeping, lets head to the hospital."

New Orleans is Calling, Hear Her??? Huh?

It was 2005, Katrina had just devastated much of the gulf coast, especially New Orleans. Her people were evacuated out of New Orleans by bus, to places they had never known and unbeknown to them at the time, with no way of coming back home. Some of these people were bused to Fort Smith, Arkansas where I was teaching Art at Dora Kimmons Junior High.

Most of my students were Hispanic, with a sprinkling of Oriental, Black and Caucasians. We had 650 different dialects and a population of 850 students. When the Katrina survivors arrived, our population grew a bit, but that wasn't the problem. Most of the survivors I taught, had an in your face attitude. One particular student of mine had been a real problem for over a week. Finally; I kept Warren after class so we could discuss a behavior plan for him. He was sitting on my stool as we were talking.

"Ok, you have been a real problem since you got here."

"So send me back!"

"No, honey, I don't want to send you back, I want to find out what is wrong, and then we can fix it. How about that?"

"Ain't nothin wrong."

"Ok, so do I have to call your mother and talk to her…" I didn't get the rest of what I was going to say out because this large boy started sobbing. All of his defenses were down and he was just a little boy again in need of help. My first thought was OMG, what have I done? I went over and put my arms around him.

"Ok honey, calm down, we can fix this, promise."

"How are you going to fix anything?" he screamed. "When Katrina hit I was in the upper ninth ward with my grandmother. We got out, I have no idea where my mother and sisters are or if they got out! They were in the lower ninth ward. You gonna fix that?"

"Yes, I am. Now stop crying." I continued to hold him for a few minutes.

"I promise you that I will find out about your mother and sisters, good, bad, or ugly. You have to promise me that when your Mother gets here you will make her proud. Deal?"

He nodded his head yes. His crying had slowed down and I handed him some Kleenex. I started wondering how I would keep my promise. He gave me a hug, all he needed was some hope. All I needed was a miracle!

"Are you ready to go back to class?" He nodded his head yes again.

"Here is a note for you to give to Mr. Comstock, OK?" I sent him out of my room and to the rest of his day. My next class had been waiting in the hallway very patiently. All of my students knew that when the door was shut and the blind was pulled down, they were to remain quiet and still.

I went home that night wondering how GD was going to solve this puzzle. My husband was working for an RV dealership in Van Buren where we lived that happened to be taking RV's to New Orleans, so the people there would have a place to stay while they were rebuilding. Perfect! "Cappy, here are the names you need to find these people in New Orleans or where they were taken. Find out everything you can about them. If they are alive, if they made it out of the lower ninth ward, please." Then I told him the story. He looked at me like I had three heads. "You have got to be kidding, right? This is a joke? You have no idea what you are asking me to do. It's impossible, Sparks really, I'm serious. It's impossible." I just stood there and smiled. I knew my Cappy and I knew he was going to do whatever he could to put this family back together. He just needed to vent.

Several weeks went by and Warren was doing beautifully in every class not just mine! He was a very intelligent student. Cappy came through and found his mother in Houston. Soon they were reunited and his Mama was proud of him. He graduated Kimmons and went to Northside High School.

When he went to Northside, we kept in touch. I wanted to make sure he was still on the right path. He had become one of my kids.

Then he came to see me for the last time. He was a junior in high school. He walked into the art room, I turned around and saw him, gave him a big hug. He was smiling ear to ear.

"I've come to say good-bye."

"Good bye? Where are you going?" His mother was behind him, with his sisters.

"Mama, the girls, and I are headed back home to New Orleans."

"Awww, I hate to see you leave, but I know you will make me proud in New Orleans as well. Keep in touch ok?"

"Mama, come to New Orleans."

"No baby, I haven't lost anything in New Orleans."

"We need you there!"

"Nope. I'll be right here, let me hear from you, here's my address and you have my phone number. Call me."

"We make promises don't we Mom Miner?' Mom Miner was only brought out if it was serious. Yes indeed, in the five years I had known him, between the two of us, we had made lots of promises. Promises to do better, to stay on the right path, etc. and it wasn't just one sided, I made promises too.

"Yes, honey we make promises."

"Ok then, promise me your will pray about it, coming to New

Orleans." We prayed together as well, for his mother and sisters, his grades, me reaching new students and making a difference, etc.

"That's not fair! Yes, I will pray about it. Not earnestly, but I will pray about it." I laughed.

"Good; cause Grand maw and I are praying you down there."

"Now that's really not fair, your grandmother is a prayer warrior!"

He gave me another hug, and he was gone. I did pray about New Orleans. I wanted to pray to stay away from New Orleans, but I prayed to do GDs will concerning her. That was March.

In October that same year, our house sold. We went to Florida to hunt a marina to live in. We were moving back on the boat. The short three years on dirt had gotten to Cappy he was water sick. We found our marina in Vero Beach. A beautiful little town on the east coast. Within walking distance from the marina was an elementary school. I talked to the principal about substituting and she was thrilled! What luck!

We went back to Arkansas packed up the house, took a lot of the stuff to the kids in KY, left our truck with them and headed back to Van Buren to get our sailboat, Navigator. Then we headed to Vero Beach. Two weeks later we were in sunny Florida! I had a job, life was good. I walked over to the school and found the principal, she immediately grabbed my arm. "Tell me you applied for a substituting position before you left to go back to Arkansas!"

"No, subs are always needed. Why?"

"Well for the first time ever, there is a hiring freeze and subs are on the list of no hires! Its four counties wide. There are no jobs here for you, well, not within a 2 hour driving radius."

"OMG! How did that happen?"

"I don't know. We have all been talking about it. I've been here over thirty years and it has never happened, its' a fluke! I am so sorry. I was looking forward to working with you. Good luck Sparkie!"

I started laughing to myself and saying "No, no, no, I am not going to New Orleans, I am not" I am sure GD was laughing too.

Every time I turned on my computer, Teach NOLA was sending

me an email! 2-3 times a day every day. They do not normally do that, just in case you are wondering.

I was stubborn, I applied for retail jobs, RV jobs, marina jobs, bar jobs, lots and lots of jobs. I was overqualified for the positons I was applying for. I finally asked a manger "Just how hard is it to run your register? I was a manager for parts and service in an RV dealership. I promise I can do this." "You will get bored." "I will get hungry before that."

I understand the clothing store; I am not a fashionista to say the least, so they were probably protecting their sales. Regardless, I did as Jonah did, I ran till I really didn't have a choice but to answer Teach NOLA.

Of course, I had an immediate answer from Teach NOLA. After several phone interviews, I was invited to New Orleans for the two days of interviews. I was asked back for the next several steps in the Teach NOLA process. In the last interview, I didn't give the canned answer, so I didn't get to New Orleans through Teach NOLA. I make it my practice to try and be honest in everything I do. I knew what they wanted me to say and why I just couldn't do it. Those words would not come out of my mouth. So, I didn't get to New Orleans through Teach NOLA. But that was certainly the beginning of the process of heading to New Orleans. My path was through Teachers-teachers. They are an organization that puts teachers with jobs all over the world.

To make a short story long, by the next school year I was teaching in New Orleans. I was teaching in Walter's beloved ninth ward!! My position was at Fredrick Douglass High School. I loved it! The students, the other teachers, it was an amazing year. But at the end of 2010, Recovery School District, closed my high school and 8 others.

I have looked for Warren but have not found him here in New Orleans. For those of you not familiar with New Orleans, it is not a big city. New Orleans is a little town, whatever you do here, will be well known here. I am sure I will find him when the time is right. I live in Treme now, which is the oldest Black Neighborhood in America. It was significant as the origin of the southern Civil Rights Movement and the birthplace of Jazz. New Orleans is my heart's home and I don't plan on leaving her again. However, with that being said I can sometimes hear God laughing. Play close attention to your Whisperers.

Folding Time

Folding time is an interesting thing. We all have been conditioned to believe that time is real and we are its slaves. Actually that's wrong. Time is a myth and we choose to believe in it! That's the truth. When I was told about folding time, UH....I didn't believe it,..... well wouldn't it be cool though, to be able to do that... but---can you really do it? Why not, RIGHT?

So the next day I was running late leaving for school. I sat in my Kia Soul, known as NOLA girl, and closed my eyes. I imagined the 25-minute trip, then I took the end of the trip and folded it back to the beginning of the trip. Like a loop. I imagined wrapping a purple rope of light around it and I said, "I will arrive at the perfect time." The rope exploded like fireworks and I figured I had done it right.

Then I left, unlike other mornings, I drove the speed limit and I didn't look at the clock. When I arrived at Angela's house, only 8 minutes had passed!

I'm not sure how it works, but I am positive it does work. I use it when I'm feeling rushed. I'm of the opinion that if I practiced it more, the results would be more profound.

Try it and see what you think. What can it hurt?

The Accidental Curse

It was late August, 2012. School was closed due to Hurricane Isaac, who was headed right for New Orleans! My son and his wife, who lived in Covington were planning a vacation out west and Sargie and I were going to stay at their house, watching the property and taking care of their two beautiful dogs.

For a while now I had the feeling that my husband was frolicking with someone else. I had no proof, just that gut feeling you get when your intuition is telling you something is desperately wrong, and you keep telling yourself everything is just fine.

The Whisperers started talking to me in my dream one night, saying "Wake up, ask him this question. So that's who it is?" At first I just started saying it in my sleep. Then the fog lifted and they repeated their instructions. I whispered, "So that's who it is?" Cappy didn't wake up. Then they said "Wake him up and ask the question loud." They really are not this demanding. It was a first for us, but I know better than to ignore them. Ok, so, I shook Cappy, he woke up. I said "So that's who it is?" He looked at me shocked and said "How did you figure it out?" I couldn't believe my ears and I was instantly livid. I don't remember all that was said, that's probably a good thing. I got out of the Vee birth, grabbed Sargent and went to the salon to sleep, taking my pillow also. Cappy got up and started gathering my clothes telling me to get off the boat now! I stopped him.

"No, its 3 in the morning. I will get off the boat in the morning, but right now I am going back to sleep."

We had a slight disagreement and after that he declared me crazy, he went back to bed. I curled up with Sargent on the salon seats. I didn't drop the table; this was enough room. We had rebuilt Navigator our 32' foot sailboat, the table dropped down to make a double bed. I wasn't in the mood. Before I went to sleep, I asked the Whisperers to wake me up at 7 so I could start moving my stuff off the boat. I went to sleep and at 7 on the nose a ray of sunshine came through the hatch and shone on my face. I woke up smiling. I knew they had my back.

I spent the morning packing my stuff off the boat and into my KIA Soul. She was stuffed. There was just enough space for Sargent to sit on the pile in the passenger seat and be comfortable. I started to leave and remembered my canvas bag of tools. Cappy was sitting on the steps to our business. I got out and started toward the steps, halfway there, he shouted "What do you think you're doing Sparkie?"

"I'm coming to get my canvas bag of tools. I had them with me 16 years ago and I am leaving with them."

"No, you are not. You go on with what you have. The tools stay here."

I stopped "Ok, if that's the way you want it." I turned around.

"That's the way it is going to be."

I started walking back to my car, I stopped, turned around and pointed my finger at him and said

"You will regret this. You end will be long, painful, and hard."

Then I turned around and continued walking to my car. Cappy and I had been together for 16 + years, married for 14, we knew each other very well. When you live together on a sailboat, on the ocean, you become almost as one. You have each other's backs and can know what the other needs without them asking. It's really strange but you have a second sense about each other and a look can mean a lot. We had this kind of communication and love between us. Then I heard

"No, come back you can take whatever you want, no worries. Take it back."

I turned around not really sure what was so terrifying to him. The look on his face said it all. He was scared. My husband, a former Marine snipper, was scared of nothing. I answered,

"Nope, you have it all, congratulations. You brought this on yourself." I turned and got in my car and left. The date was August 28th, 2012. Hurricane Isaac hit early the next morning. (I didn't realize I had pronounced a curse on Cappy till I had relayed the story to Shaman John. He thought it was funny that I didn't know I was putting a curse on him.)

I drove to my son's house in Covington. I drove in his driveway that afternoon. I didn't unpack the car, just left it in the driveway. Sargie and I walked in and settled in. That night it was just windy, on the TV I watched Hurricane Isaac shift and move to come ashore. He settled right over Slidell, LA. He was right over the Marina! (Just a side note here that I thought was very interesting, my great grandfather's name was Isaac Messer. His Spirit has been with me my entire life. But that also is another story, named Isaac.)

In Covington, we never lost power, never had much rain, and it was comfortable, however the Marina was flooded, along with our business and my truck.

Cappy and I had now officially separated. I started looking for places to move into. I called The American Can it is an apartment complex in Mid City. Mid City was also suffering from Hurricane Isaac. They were without power. I had an appointment with the manager. I walked in and filled out the paperwork. I wanted to see the apartment. I was told no, because of the power outage the elevators didn't work, I told them I didn't care I need a place to go move into. She would not let me and couldn't get me an apartment till the next week. That would not do I needed a place to stay before

Jay and Heather got home. I was in a panic. Then I settled myself and asked where I needed to go. I was told River Ridge. I had no idea where that was. I put it into my GPS and went to River Ridge. There was an apartment complex that was renting units. I stopped at the manager's office, saw and rented an apartment. I was moved in before Jay and Heather got home. Their hospitality was a true gift that was a help beyond measure.

Walking Sargent Major

In 2012, while living in River Ridge, an outlying district of New Orleans, I had a West Highland Terrier whose name was Sargent Major. He was a very smart little dog. I lived in an apartment complex. I wasn't thrilled to live there but it was the only place that was available after Hurricane Isaac blew through Grand Isles and Mid City causing power outages and flooding. That is another story named The Curse!

When Sargie and I went for our walk this morning, the sun was shining brilliantly and there was a slight breeze. As I stepped off the sidewalk onto the street, the scenery changed greatly!

In an instant, I was in fog, heavy dense fog. I started looking around. I was leaving a dense forest to my back and I was close to a river bank! I looked at down and saw my shoes. They were felt, a dark gray. I noticed that I was wearing a long dress that was also a muted color, and I had a hooded cape around me. The hood was up. I had long hair on my shoulders. As I was standing there, I tried to take in all the information I could because I felt it may not last long. Sargie was not with me in this space! I could see and hear Crow, that wasn't unusual, Crows is always with me. He is one of my Spirit Animals. As I started asking what the meaning of this was, Sargie made his presence known tugging me back and I was again in 2012

71

standing with one foot on the sidewalk and the other lifted to step onto the street!

Well, that was an interesting way to start my day. I finished Sargie's walk and went to school. Needless to say I could not shake the whatever it was that morning. When I got home, I contacted Shaman John in California. I told him about what happened that morning.

"Well Medicine Woman Sparkie, if I were you I would do some research on River Ridge at the time period you think you might have been in. Obviously, you were there in that time period. My bet is River Ridge was named that because of a river near there. You must have lived near the river and I would lay money on the fact that at that time, you were tagged as a witch or conjurer. Crow has been with you a long time; you know that right?"

"Yes, ever since I can remember, I have always had a crow with me. Squawking hello, watch out, and other things."

"Wait, you know what Crow is saying?" Shaman John was chuckling then. I wasn't sure what was so funny.

"Yes, and I talk back to him. Why are you laughing?"

"Of course you do, that doesn't surprise me at all. Not at all. You have a lot of power around you, and you are not even aware of it yet. You will be you in a transition. Keep studying and listening. Your Crow has gone through many lifetimes with you, which is why you can talk to him now. It wasn't always like that for you."

"Wow, I just thought it was a gift I was given as a child."

"Yes, he is a gift given to you when you were a child in every life time you have been in. He is here to provide insight and supporting your intentions. He brings luck with him. He is here to support you in developing the power of sight, transformation, and connection with life's magic. He helps you with higher perspective, being fearless, flexibility, and alchemy. He's a very special Spirit Animal. It doesn't surprise me that you have him either."

When we hung up, I had more questions than answers. My research had started.

What I found out was the area known as River Ridge was developed by French colonists and their descendants in the late 18th centuries for large sugar plantations; these lined the Mississippi River in traditional French long-lot fashion. Having done my DNA, I do know that I have some French background in my DNA, not that it proves I was here then, but being able to see where I lived at the time, for me certainly does.

If you have had this happen to you, don't be afraid. You are not crazy, you are being shown what few people ever get to see, a glimpse of who you were and where you have been. Treasure it! Not everyone gets that opportunity!

Roller Derby Queen

I often have dreams that are so vivid, I have no problem remembering them. When vivid dreams happen, I have learned to start looking around my dream for details. I try to remember all I can about my surroundings, the people, what they are wearing, and what I am doing. I do this because when they are that vivid, they will be coming true and I want to make sure that I am aware of what will happen and what will be said.

Fredrick Douglass High School in New Orleans was closed by the Recovery School District in 2010. I was teaching there and loved it. This high school was in the 9th ward. The RSD closed 8 other schools as well, but I took this personally. I had been asking the man in charge for the last six months of the school year if we were closing. I could have gotten a heads up on a new job if that was the case. He kept telling me no, right up to the last week of school, when he called all the teachers together to let us know that they were closing the high school right after graduation! I was having a problem finding a job especially with that many schools closing and that many teachers out of jobs, all of us scrambling for jobs.

I was continually getting offered positions in Nashville, TN. It reminded me of when I was in Vero Beach, FL and kept getting notices from Teach NOLA.

"Sparkie, have you gotten any job offers?"

"No, just from Metro Nashville. I don't want to leave New Orleans, Cappy."

"Well, that will put us closer to John David, Jay and Sarah. Who knows maybe this is like the Teach NOLA thing? Maybe you are supposed to be there for some unknown reason. Answer it, if you are not supposed to be there, you know as well as I do that we will not be moving. But if you are, we can get a heads up on a place to live. Give it a try."

What does one say to that? I know all of the time I wasted running from New Orleans and how difficult it became for me to get a job there. It would have been so much easier for us if I had just given in the first time Teach NOLA came up.

What the heck. I applied for the position. I was called for a phone interview. Then I was called for an interview.

We drove from New Orleans to Bowling Green, KY, about an hour north of Nashville to my daughter Sarah's house and spent the night. I drove with Sarah to see how to get to the school and what it looked like. The campus was really nice, lots of grass areas and no chain link fence. The night before my interview, I made paper paws to give to the students that I would be teaching. These would be given out to students that could answer the questions correctly. I got to the school early. I met the principal and we chatted a bit. Another teacher was teaching a lesson and I was next. I asked the principal, who was scoring the teaching if she was in there talking to me. "Oh my Seniors are scoring the teachers. It will be their legacy to the juniors and underclassmen to pick a really good teacher. Personally I thought that was a fantastic idea. I was called next. I walked down the hallway with a very personable Senior.

"So, what are your plans when you graduate? Do you have plans for more education?"

He looked at me strangely. "Aren't you supposed to ask me what college I am going to?"

"Well I suppose if you are planning on going to college, but honestly college isn't for everyone. You know that plumbers and electricians make really good money. For that you need a vocational school or an apprenticeship. I was just wondering if you had future plans. If you have thought about it? I wasn't allowed to think about the future when I graduated high school. I was told I had to go to college. Just being nosey."

He laughed. We had been in the hallway talking for a few minutes. He was picking my brain. "Well do you see votech as being less than college? Do you think it makes you less of an intelligent person?"

"Absolutely not. I believe it makes you a focused person."

He grinned and we went into the classroom. I walked to the blackboard and wrote. Sparkie Miner. Then I wrote on the board; Please, on the paper given to you, list what qualities you are looking for in an art teacher. Where you see your future going and why. Please put you name at the top right corner of the paper. Then I handed out stacks of paper to each roll.

I put down all the materials and bags I had come with and started sorting them out. I was ready to teach. "Good morning! My name is Sparkie Miner. I am here to teach you an art lesson. Since I do not know anyone's name, I decided to set up a rewards system. These are panther paws, the more you receive the better your chances of getting the final prize." I showed the candy that would be the final prize and the pieces of hard candy that would be given for participation and of course the panther paws.

I taught my lesson and we had a great time. I handed out all of the panther paws and gave out candy. Then everyone put their names on the back of the panther paws and I put them in a box. Shook them up and had my former escort to pull out one paw. He did and the final prize was given to the winner. This student shared with all of the other students.

I was then escorted back to the office.

"We will call you and let you know one way or the other about the position. It was good to meet you."

"You as well, I will wait for your call. Thank you. You have an exceptional group of students in there. I am sure they will do a great job for you." And I walked out the door, back into the sunshine. I was walking along and closed my eyes so I could feel the sun on my face.

"Mrs. Miner!! Mrs. Miner!!" I looked around an out of the windows were the students, waving at me. "We love you!"

I placed my hand over my heart, bowed my head in respect and answered. "I love you all too. GD will bless you as you go through life."

"Come to our graduation PLEASE!"

"Of course, when is it?"

"Tomorrow night, in the gym, at 7:00."

"I'll be there. Now you all get back to work." I left the school laughing at what just happened. I drove back to my daughter's house in Bowling Green. On the way back my phone rang. "Mrs. Miner, you made a huge impression on our Seniors, you have the job. I was to inform you that there will be two tickets for you and your husband at the graduation ceremony tomorrow night. You will be sitting on the side with the teachers. This is really never happened before but they want you there and it is their graduation."

"I'll be there."

When I got back to KY, my husband was waiting for me. "Well, any word?" "Yes, I am hired and we are going to the graduation tomorrow night." He laughed.

Just before we moved, I had a most vivid dream. I was working with a roller derby queen! I had never ever known anyone who was in the roller derby! I was so excited!

When I got to my new school, I started asking everyone if they were in the roller derby. I immediately was labeled as a crazy woman from New Orleans. So, I stopped asking. I stayed at Maplewood High School for one year, but I knew in September, this was not the school for me. I was unhappy and at the end of the year, we headed back to New Orleans.

I didn't have a job, but I knew I was going to have one. When we moved into the marina, I started looking at the want ads. I found a position for an after school coordinator at Morris Jeff Elementary. I applied. I got an interview and during the interview I got the position of long term substitute teacher of art. It seems that the Art teacher was sick and would not be back for a long time.

I didn't ask anyone about being a roller derby queen, after the disastrous results I got in Nashville. I just did my jobs and minded my own business. I was fixing the computers in the library one day when I overheard the librarian ask her assistant "How did you get that bruise again?" "I was in the rink last night and got run over. I got knocked down, but I got up and on the next round, I took her out! The crowd started yelling Roller Derby Queen!" I dropped my book and started laughing. I walked over to them. "Excuse me, I couldn't help but overhear you say you were in the roller derby. Is that correct?" "Yes, it is and last night the crowd yelled "Roller Derby Queen!" I just laughed and smiled. I knew I was in the right place. This is where I was supposed to be. "I dreamed about you a year ago. So glad to meet you."

My time at Morris Jeff was always fun and Sarah, who was the assistant is now the librarian there. Red headed and beautiful inside and out.

You must remember that things don't always work as we think they will or on the timetable we set up for them. This was the longest time between a dream and it becoming reality that I knew of at the time. It was a learning process for me. I know now that it will come in it's on perfect time.

My First Manifestation

My first manifestation took place on May 29th, 2013. Bayou Boogaloo was taking place. It is in Mid City in New Orleans and is always full of fun, music, arts and crafts and people on the water. What a fantastic three days! I had gone with my friend Sandra to listen to the music and see the sites. We could park at her mother's house and walk over. There were people on their own floatation devices on the bayou. Some of them were fantastic, others were creative and I personally liked the ones that had a hard time staying above water for whatever reason. The music could be heard long before you reached the bayou. Alcoholic beverages were sold along with water and fountain drinks. People were dressed in the most amazing outfits.

One artist I saw, was creating works of art out of cement! He had little fairies, and large garden faces. There were heads that could shoot water out like a fountain and a number of other things. I was intrigued. But went on to see other sites and artwork. I bought a pair of earrings that were made from beetle's wings! They were stunning. Shimmered in blues and greens. At the end of the night, we headed out and for home. As I passed the cement man again, I stopped and bought a garden face, even though I didn't have a garden and two of the small fairies. I asked him to wrap the fairies separately and he did so. One fairy was for my friend Susan who didn't come with us and the other for me. They were identical and very cool.

When I got back to the car that night, I noticed that I only had one fairy. I unwrapped it to make sure he didn't put the two together. No such luck! I wrapped the other fairy back up in the newspaper she was in. Nope just one fairy. I kept repeating, "Nothing is hidden from God's eyes." Holding to the fact that I would find the other fairy. I fully expected to find her, wherever she went.

"Let's go back and look for her Sparkie. I am sure you just dropped her on the way home."

"Ok, maybe so."

We didn't find her and we gave up. "You know Sandra that fairies go where they want to go most of the time. I hope she has found a fantastic home." It was ok, I still had the one to give to Susan and I knew she would love it. I didn't think about mine anymore, and again wished her a happy place to be.

A week later, I saw Susan. "I have a surprise for you that I got when I went to Bayou Boogaloo." And I handed Susan the newspaper wad. As she started to open it I said "There were two fairies to start with, one for you and one for me. I even had them wrapped separately, but I lost one on the way to the car. "Oh Sparkie, I am so sorry, you can have this one." Then she gasped, and looked at me strangely "What?" "Sparkie, how many fairies were wrapped up?" "Only one because I asked him to wrap them separately and he did. I didn't want to have to unwrap it and then wrap it back up again. Why?"

She started to laugh and held up two fairies. One was on the top of the other one and they were different.! "I am sure you are mistaken about having them wrapped separately."

When I got to school the next day I stopped Sandra, there were a lot of other teachers around. "I wanted to ask you about the fairies that I got at the festival this past weekend." "Ok, sure what do you want to know?" "When I bought them, did you see how they were wrapped?" "Yes, they were wrapped separately, why?"

"Hang with me, nobody leave; I want witnesses. So what happened to the fairies?"

"You lost one on the way to the car. We went back and looked for it but didn't find it. You said fairies go where they want to when they want to and you hoped it had a happy home." "Right that's the way I remember it too. Were the fairies different or alike or do you remember?" "They were identical which I thought was not all that. Yours should have been the other fairy there and I told you that at the time. It looked like you." "Yes you did. Ok everyone with me?"

"Sandra, is this the fairy I gave Susan?" Looking at the picture she said "Yes. It is boring like her." Then she laughed.

I held up the fairy that I had, "have you seen this fairy?" "Yes, that's the one that looks like you. Did you go back and get it? Wait, no you couldn't have because we left at closing. Where did you get this one?"

"SOOOO, I gave Susan hers last night when she opened it, there was this fairy on top of the other fairy. Wrapped together."

"That's not possible! I watched him wrap both boring fairies up separately!"

"I know right! What did I tell you about fairies?" I was glad my fairy came home to me. I have her hanging by the door as a reminder when I leave, that our world is a wonderfully mysterious place, and that fairies go where they want to when they want to!

Barley

My 10-year-old granddaughter came to spend the summer with me in 2013. It was a very eventful summer, although it started out very lazy! Gwynivere and I spent the days lounging by the pool, swimming and talking, going to movies, walking around the French Quarter, and enjoying our time together. At night after supper we would go back to the pool and very quietly swim till 11 pm., several hours after the pool was closed.

In the middle of our time together, I had to be in Austin, TX. For training. So I packed up my two dogs Barley, a wire haired Dachshund, Sargent, my Westie, Miss Gwynivere, and headed to Tennessee. My oldest son said I could drop them all off at his house while I was in Austin. Then I would fly out of Nashville instead of New Orleans. That got me a cheaper flight. But I'm getting ahead of myself. We uneventfully made it to Christiana.

I let the dogs out of the car and Barley started running around crazy. The first place he headed was to the road. He didn't come when called, and started playing catch me if you can! When I finally caught him we were both tired. I was ready to kill him. I told him I was going to put him in the fenced in backyard. I walked to the fence with Gwynivere, holding Barley and fussing at him. Inside the fence were Barley's brothers and sister. A pitbull and two dachshunds. After petting the other dogs through the fence, talking to them, and letting them sniff Barley, I dropped him over the fence. Everything was great while he was on the outside of the fence. Rupert even licked his head. But as soon as I dropped Barley over the fence, Rupert, my son's pit bull which had grown up with Barley from a puppy, picked him up by his head and started shaking him!! I screamed at the dog to stop and started to run from the side yard to the house. I ran through the house to the backyard. By this time Rupert had made it to the patio, he still had Barley by the head and was still shaking him. Barley looked like a little rag doll. There was no resistance! He was just limp! I grabbed Ruperts head with one hand and putting my left hand in his mouth, I tried to get Barley's head out, with no luck at all. Neither one of us was letting go!! Gwynivere came out with a broom and hit Rupurt over the head with the handle several times with all her might before he released Barley. Barley was limp. I took his little lifeless body into the house. He was covered with blood. As I checked him over, I discovered that he had no bites anywhere, I was the one bleeding!

"Grandmaw, your bleeding, is Barley ok?" "Gwyn honey, you saved his life, hitting Rupert so hard. It's my little finger, can you go get me a washcloth?" Sending her away gave me a chance to look at Barley, his eyes were foggy as he tried to see me, then they rolled back into his head and he was gone. "No, you are not dying on me!" I closed my eyes and imagined white healing light going from my hands into his body through his head. This light was taking away all the shock and injuries that I saw. I started at his brain, worked my way through his body, fixing what I saw wrong as I went. His heart was not working, so I restarted it. Then I saw that his lungs were not working so I restarted them. There were several broken ribs, and other things that I saw wrong and had fixed. I filled him with white light paste after I had worked on all the things that I saw wrong with him. I opened my eyes and looked at this sweet little dog lying lifeless in my hands. "All Father, I ask that you put the life spark back into Barley. This was my fault and I take full responsibility for it. He does not deserve to die like this." Then with a jerk, and a sudden gasp of air, his eyes flew open and he looked at me like – "What did you do?" He sighed deeply. At that time Gwynivere came back with the washcloth. I was hugging Barley and talking to him crying as I did. "Don't worry buddy, I wasn't going to let you die like that, I love you."

Gwynivere looked at me and Barley astonished. "Wait, he's not dead? Grandmaw he looked dead. What did you do?" She handed me the washcloth. I wrapped up my little finger on my left hand with a paper towel and put the washcloth around it. "No, baby, he's not dead. But we are going to take him to the vet just to make sure he is ok." "Oh Grandmaw I am so happy." She reaches over and pets Barley on his head. "Call your mother and to tell her we are headed to the vet and why." Dushawn was down the street visiting her sister. Gwyn looked at me while holding the phone, "We needed to wait for her to get home." "No, that is not going to happen, we can stop and pick her up on the way to the vet." Dushawn was standing in the middle of the road, she left her car at her sister's house and got in. I was driving with Barley in my lap, which doesn't sound difficult until you figure in that my car is not an automatic. Dushawn looked at my hand and said, "You got bit?" "Yes, and I am not sure who did it, I had my hand in Rupert's mouth, so my fault, not his." "If you tell the doc that, they will want to pin up the dogs for 30 days for rabies or put Rupert down." "Wow, well, maybe I just cut it on the chain link fence." We drove the rest of the way in silence. I did not want to be responsible for all of that mess and we know that neither dog has rabies. Hummm.

We pulled into the vets parking lot, which was full. I was carrying Barley as we walked into the office. There were a lot of people waiting there. Dushawn started talking to the receptionist, telling her what happened. She didn't ask questions she just took us immediately back to a room. I thought they were being quite efficient, with all the people in the waiting room. She closed the door and said the doctor would be right here. I was still holding Barley and talking to him. "Everything's going to be alright, buddy. The doctor will be here in a minute." The doctor came in. "Barley on the table, please." I reluctantly did. As we were explaining what happed he examined Barley. "I don't find anything wrong with him. He has a few sore ribs, but other than that, I don't find anything. The blood on his nose isn't his. I would like to keep him till this afternoon. You can pick him up about four."

Then the doctor looked at me "You need to get to a hospital." "Naw, I have a cut on my little finger, they tend to bleed a lot." "So, the dog bit you?" "No, I cut it on the chain link fence." "You sure?" "Yes, sir I am."

"You haven't looked at yourself have you??"

"No why? Really I'm alright."

"Sure you are, umm hum, look down, you can use my sink out there to clean up in. Wouldn't want anyone to rush you into surgery."

I was confused, so I looked down, and what I saw would have scared me if I didn't know that I was ok. It was summer, I had on shorts and a tee shirt that was covered in blood, my own. Blood was all down my legs and all over my arms and feet, because I had no shoes on. I looked like something out of a horror movie.

"Dushawn, help her get the blood off her face and out of her hair." Dushawn laughed and came over to me. "Mom, you really do look bad." We both laughed. "I guess I do, I didn't realize how much blood I had on me."

After I cleaned up, the doctor came over. "Thank you for looking at Barley on such short notice and for letting me clean up." He nodded his head, reached for my hand and took off the washcloth and the paper towel. Then he looked at me "Well I'd say 3-4 stiches would take care of it." I then looked at my finger. Ok, so it probably need a stich or two. "So can you stitch it up here?" He laughed and "No, there is an urgent care walk in type clinic over by Kroger's." "So I have a question, we got back so quickly because I looked like I had been attacked, not because you all are so efficient?" He just laughed and nodded yes. That explained a lot. As we walked through the whispering people in the waiting room. I had to laugh, I just looked at them and said "Really I'm ok and so is my dog." That just increased the whispering. We left Barley and went in search of the walk in clinic.

We walked into the Urgent Care, together. I went to the receptionist, and said "I cut my finger on a chain link fence and I think I need some stiches." However, they looked at me like I needed a hospital. They took me straight back. I had not filled out anything or signed any papers. I am assuming having blood stains all over my shirt and shorts, qualified me as an emergency. Once in a room the receptionist came with the paperwork. Dushawn took all of the cards out of my wallet for her and I signed a paper for treatment. "The doctor will be right in. So this happened on a chain link fence right?" "Yes ma'am." Then she smiled and walked out. I started wondering what kind of an example I was setting for my granddaughter. "Grandmaw, don't worry about me, I think it's right what we are doing. Thank you." Hummm, that really gave me pause.

Then the doc came in. "Well Ms. Miner, what exactly happened to your finger?" He asked as he was looking at it. I knew I didn't have Barley's rabies records with me and I knew that I would have to take rabies shots. Two weeks prior to this Rupert had killed a dog while my son was holding him in his arms and lacerated John's forearm. Because he didn't have Rupert's rabies records with him, he had to take a series of rabies shots. Nope that was not going to happen. "I caught it on the top of a chain link fence." "Really?" "Yes, sir." "Are you allergic to any medications?" "Yes, codeine, lidocaine, and oxycodone." When the doc came back, he looked at my finger again. "I can give you anything for the pain, but the shot will hurt worse than sewing it up." "I know; can I have a sucker?" "No Grandmaw, meditate, put yourself somewhere beautiful, near the ocean." "Good idea, baby girl." The doc didn't know what to think. "Ok doc, give me a couple of minutes and start." He looked at me like I had lost my mind. "Ok" So, I put myself on a beautiful beach and I did not feel the shot go in. Gwyn came over and touched my arm, "Grandmaw it's all over." "Aww thank you." We all chatted will we were waiting for the doc to come back and sew up my finger.

The doc was very nice. "How are your sons?" He looked at me strangely. "They have both been sick but are much better today. "How did you know that?" I just grinned "They are going to be fine." He finished sewing me up and told me to come back in 10 days to take the stitches out. "Can I take them out myself?" He laughed and said "Be sure you get them all out, OK?" "Sure." "Say, will it be alright for me to drive back to New Orleans in the AM?" "Sure, I see no problem." "Great, it's just 8.5 hours." Then Dushawn nudged me, "Tell him." "Oh I drive a stick." "Of course you do. With an automatic, you could do it no worries, but a stick, NO. You could tear out the stitches really easily and then we would really have a problem. I had to cut the incision straight because it was jagged like a dog bite. If you pull out the stitches, there will be no way to sew it back up. Sorry."

Later that afternoon we picked up Barley. He was very glad to see us and was jumping and making whining noises. He sat on my lap, licking me. He didn't have a scratch on him, but he was sore. I'll bet he was! I held him till time for bed. He was milking it, but I didn't care.

The next day, I swapped flights, leaving from Nashville instead of New Orleans and returning to Nashville. Dushawn lent me some clothes and all was right with the world. I was off to Austin!!

<…….>

Cappy's Passing

I was in Christiana, Tennessee, visiting my granddaughter Gwynivere and her parents. I was sleeping with Gwyn in her bed. I had chosen the side by the door. I was soundly sleeping, when I could feel myself being shaken awake! Why don't they stop shaking me? I woke with a start. Is everything ok? Where am I? Looking around I realized where I was, oh yes at John David's. I could hear Gwyn softly breathing. I swung my feet over the edge of the bed and looked at the clock 3:39. Wow. Rubbing my eyes trying to figure out what was going on, I saw a movie reel, playing right before my eyes. A man with blonde hair, his head between his hands and bent over. Then suddenly, I saw the picture of bubbles coming out of the back of his head!! I screamed "NO!" and started trying to push the bubbles back into his head. Then it was gone and I was left crying and looking into the dark hallway. I was still sitting on the side of Gwynivere's bed. I had come for a visit for the weekend. School for me wasn't out till July and this was the middle of June! I got up and rushed into John and Dushawn's bedroom, just to make sure John was alright. He no longer has blonde hair but to me he will always be that towheaded little boy. As I entered their room, the bathroom light was on and I could see John David sound asleep and snoring. Relief come over me. I walked to the doorway of the bathroom and saw Dushawn cleaning on her hands and knees, she looked up as I came to the doorway. "Are you alright?" Then she turned around, "OMG, no you are not alright." She got up and came over to me. "What's wrong Mom?" The look on her face made me realize that I must look affright. She put her arm around me and walked me into the family room, kitchen combination. She fixed me a cup of hot chocolate and handed me the cup. "What are you doing up at this hour cleaning the bathroom?" "John David was sick and he got up and made a mess, I'm cleaning it up." "Oh ok." "Well tell me why you are up, what is going on?" I told Dushawn what had happened. "And you thought it was John David? You know you only know one blonde headed man, right?" "Yes, I know. But John David will always be my little towheaded boy. Lordy, so you think it is Cappy?" "Yes, we can call it's 4:10, He'd still be up." "No, if he's awake, a drunk Cappy isn't always a happy Cappy. If he's asleep, that will be a blessing to whomever he is with." We both laughed. After 16 years of marriage, we both knew it was a crap shoot as to his mental condition at that time of the morning. I finished my hot chocolate and we both went back to bed. I didn't have to call. I knew he had passed and I would learn of it soon enough. Cappy was my husband, and I laid awake and remembered the good times we had sailing all over.

Later that afternoon, I got a call from my brother-in-law. After we exchanged hellos. "Are you sitting down?" "Yes" I was actually standing by the bed in Gwyn's room. I was waiting to hear that my 94-year-old father-in-law had passed, just wishful thinking.

"Cappy died this morning."

"What time did he pass?"

"What?"

"What time did he pass? Do you know the time?"

"3:30"

"Well, no wonder he was pissed off. It took him 9 minutes to find me in the ethers. He came to see me this morning, 9 minutes after he passed. He had a hard time waking me up too."

"You know I don't believe that stuff, right."

"Yes, but it doesn't mean it isn't true. You see it doesn't depend on you believing it to make it so. I'm sorry for your loss. Is there anything I can do? How are his Dad and Jenny doing?"

"Maybe you should call them"

"OK."

I hung up the phone, went into the kitchen. "Cappy passed this morning at 3:30 am. Joel just called and confirmed it."

Dushawn looked at me and said "No wonder he was pissed; he didn't make it here till 3:39."

One has to love digital clocks.

(The picture at the beginning of this is exactly what I saw coming out of his head, that I was trying to push back in.) I didn't find the picture till years later, when I did I sat there with my mouth open. So I know I am not the only one who has seen this.

RIP

ROBERT HOWARD MINER

1-5-43 TO 6-15-13

Finding an Urn

After finding out my husband had died while in Florida on our boat, I also found out from our attorney that the divorce proceedings had been stopped by Cappy (my late husband). Our attorney Ben had been told that we were working things out and were not getting a divorce. No one bothered to tell me that. I was under the impression that our divorce was final in November of 2012. It was now June 2013. OMG!! I am responsible for him because we are still technically still married!! Good Lord! While I was pondering all of this, my phone rang. "Hi, this is J.R. You are Robert's x-wife correct?"

"Actually, No. I am Cappy's wife of 16 years. How can I help you?"

"You can give me his dog. He loved that dog and I want it." "Ummm, well that is not going to happen. I have had Sargent Major for the last 14 years and I do not intend to give him to you." I hung up. The phone rang again,

"Well you are not his wife, you all were divorced in November."

"See that is exactly what I thought until I talked to our attorney. Who you called and he told you exactly what he told me. Cappy told him we were getting back together and there would be no divorce.

So Ben did not file the papers in November. I just found out about this as well. So it was a shock to me too."

"No, I am looking at the papers right here." I hung up this was going nowhere and I needed a cup of coffee. My phone rang again. It was Ricky, Cappy's oldest and dearest friend. "Sparkie, you have to do something. J.R. is going to just dump Cappy's ashes in the ocean and nobody gets to say goodbye." "Ricky what do you want me to do?"

"Call the morgue and get the ashes."

"Fine do you know where the morgue is or what the name of the morgue is?"

"No." I hung up and called Ben.

"Ben, do you know where Cappy's ashes are? How do I get them? His friends want to have a memorial for him." Ben told me where his body was and reminded me that I was his wife and responsible for taking care of the memorial and his ashes. So I called the morgue in Florida.

"Good morning this is blah blah, how can I assist you?"

"This is Sparkie Miner; I believe you have my husband. He died on his boat?"

"Ummmm, what is your husband's name ma'am?"

"Robert Howard Miner, he died yesterday morning at 3:30 am." There was a long pause, then a string of curse words. After using the f word several times, "Shit, yes ma'am we have Robert. Can I ask for your full name, address, and how long you were married and where?"

"Sure." I gave her all the information and asked if I needed to send her our marriage certificate. We were married in St. Augustine and I was sure our Rabbi would vouch for the wedding if she needed to talk to him.

"Shit, no, I don't need to talk to him. I just need to fix the paperwork on Robert, would you mind helping me with that?" "Sure"

"Who is J.R.? I have her listed as his next of kin."

I laughed, "Well, she is his current girlfriend." The cursing started again with

"I knew it; I just knew it!" She kept telling me she had no idea he was married. I laughed and said "I can't imagine why his girlfriend didn't tell you that." We got all of the paperwork straightened out and then she said,

"Robert has been taken to the funeral home. I'll be glad to give you their number."

"Great, thank you."

This just kept getting better and better. I called the funeral home and got almost the same reaction as the lady in the morgue. Finally, she said,

"He hasn't been cremated yet, his daughter is paying for that. I need your physical address so I can mail his ashes to you. The ashes have to go to the next of kin." She kept apologizing about having to fix the paperwork correctly. I told her it was not problem for me. "I wasn't told he was married." "I know, J.R. didn't tell anyone that. It's ok really." She agreed to send me the death certificate and his ashes. I gave her my address and hung up.

Now I needed to call Jennifer, his daughter. We had a very pleasant conversation and I asked her about a memorial. We agreed that I needed to talk to his parents. When I called them, the reception was not very warm and I gave up on that. My phone rang again.

"Hi, Jennifer what's up?"

"I want Dad's ashes; they will only send them to his next of kin which is you. Will you send them to me?"

"Yes, honey as soon as I get them and after the service here I will send them to you. Do you want to come here for the service? It will be a small one in the synagogue. You are welcome."

"No, I'll have one up here for him."

Cappy had called me in May and asked me to make sure if anything happened to him, that I would get him a Jewish funeral. I had told him at the time that he actually needed to be Jewish for that to happen."

"You'll do that for me because you love me and I know that."
Yes, I did love him, just couldn't live with him.

I called a good friend of mine.

"Angela, boy have I got a story for you! Want to go to the quarter with me, I have something I have to purchase?"

"Sure, what are we shopping for?"

"I'll tell you when I get there. But you are not going to believe this girl!!"

"OOOkkkk."

I picked her up about twenty minutes later and I explained what was going on. I was right she didn't believe it; she was shocked but agreed that it sounded just like Cappy.

"When's he gonna get here? Where are we going to find a box like you want?"

"He'll be here the end of the week and I am not sure where I'll find the box, but I am sure the Whisperers will tell me."

I was driving down Charters looking for a place to park. It's a pretty centrally located place, and I assumed we would be looking for a while. I spotted a place and started to back into it, I was having a bit of a problem, when a tall man in a cowboy hat came out of the store.

"Hold on little lady, I'll move my big ole truck and you will have no problem!" He got in his red truck and left. I pulled into the spot, looked at Angela and said "This may take a while, hope you have on your walking shoes." She just laughed.

As I got out of the car, locked it, looked at the store we parked in front of I heard "This is it. They have his box."

"Angela, this is the place, I was just told." She just looked at me and smiled. "OK. That didn't take long."

We walked into a dark, long narrow shop. Much like a shotgun house. Probably was in its earlier life. It was stuffed full of glass shelves, with beautiful crystal everywhere. There were a few paintings but mostly crystal everything. As I looked around, I didn't see any boxes. But I was sure this was where the box was. In the center of the shop, there was a desk with a young black man sitting behind it exquisitely dressed, he spoke with an accent that I could not place.

"What can I do to help you?"

"I'm here to get the box."

He was shocked and asked me to repeat what I said, this time he had no accent.

"I am here to get the box."

"Ma'am, we don't have any boxes as you can see we sell crystal."

"Yes you do, it's about this size." I motioned with my hands how large I thought it should be.

He got up "Follow me." He started walking to the back of the shop without saying a word. He went behind the counter, reached to the side and pulled out a stationary holder.

"No, that's not the one, It's smaller than that. It's the other one."

Frustrated he opened a cabinet door to his right, and pulled out the most beautifully decorated box I had ever seen. It was Egyptian design and showed a woman holding up a light to the heavens, like giving a soul away.

"Oh, that's beautiful. That's the one, yes that is the one for sure."

"How did you know this box was here? It just arrived from Egypt this am and it isn't even in the system yet! How did you know??"

I stood there and grinned. Should I tell him or act like I was lucky?

"The Whisperers told me. They gave me the parking place out front too. I need it for an urn. Since it isn't in the system yet, and I don't have the ashes yet, can you put my name on it and I'll be back to pick it up when the ashes get here at the end of the week? I just need to make sure it's large enough. They should be here by Friday."

He was dumb founded. He just nodded his head and wrote my name and information on a piece of paper and the agreed price.

We walked out and Angela was just staring at me.

"Sparkie, really, how did you know that?"

"The Whisperers told me, that's how I knew. He seemed a little shaken up huh?"

"Well yeah, can I come back with you, that should be fun too?" And she started to laugh.

Well Friday came and my mail lady knocked on my door. She handed me the paper to sign for the box. I signed the papers and she handed me the box. As she was handing me the box she said very meekly… "That's not what I think it is……is it?"

"Oh, I am so sorry. Cappy this is my mail lady; this is Cappy."

"Oh Lord lady you is crazy!" Grabbing the card, she ran down the two flights of stairs. I started laughing and told Cappy he shouldn't scare nice women. I went inside and called Angela. She was more than ready for this trip.

We took Cappy with us to see if he would indeed fit into the box we had negotiated for him.

The gentleman that waited on us before recognized us when we came in. He grinned and we walked with him to the back of the store not saying a word. Looking at the box Cappy was in and the box we were purchasing we decided he would fit. Great. I paid for the box. The gentleman said "Are those the remains of your dog or favorite pet?"

I laughed.

"Umm, no not exactly, how bout a cheating husband who died with his girlfriend?"

Once again he was blown out of the water.

"Oh, Lord, dats whose in dat box?" His accent long forgotten and fear was all that remained.

"Oh, my bad, Cappy this is…. I'm sorry, I don't know your name."

"Gerald." He said meekly and softly. Looking at me like he had no idea what I was going to do next.

"Ok, Gerald, what a lovely name, this is Gerald, Gerald, this is Cappy."

"Ya all leavin now cause, it's about time for you to leave, right?"

"Sure Gerald, thank you again for all your help."

We walked through the store and out into the bright sunshine. Gerald however, I don't think will ever be the same.

When we got into the car, Angela looked at me.

"You know you have to stop playing with people and Cappy. You might have scared that boy for life." "I'm sorry, you're right, I have been bad, but I haven't had this much fun with Cappy in years. Then we both laughed. We went to the nearest bar in the Quarter and had two Bloody Mary's. That was how all of 2013 was for me, quite eventful.

Getting a 504 Number

On August 22nd of 2013, I decided I had been in New Orleans long enough to have a 504 New Orleans area code and number. Angela and I went to the T Mobile store. "Welcome to T Mobile. What can we help you with today?" "I would like to change my 479 number to a 504 number." "Sure that's not a problem, follow me." We were taken to the back of a long store and were seated at a desk. The woman was on the phone. It was almost closing. She hung up "Now, you said you wanted a 504 number, correct?"

"Yes that is correct."

She got into her computer and wrote down a number "Ok, this is your new number, Is there anything else I can help you with?"

I reached across the desk and turned her computer screen so I could see it.

"I don't want this number. I will never be able to remember that number. Let me see......." I looked at the long list of number available. Then one jumped out at me. "That number, I want that number."

The woman looked at me like I had lost my mind.

"What?" It all had happened in a split second before she really realized what I had done. But it was almost closing and I am sure she wanted to go home so instead of telling me that I cannot one, touch her computer and two pick my own number, however, she just grinned. I don't think anyone had ever done that to her.

"Sure what the hell. Are you sure 504 617 0166 is the number you want because once you pick it you will not be able to change it. You positive?"

I knew that wasn't the case, but I acted like it was and I just nodded. She typed on her keyboard and then looked up. "Alright Ms. Miner, that is now your official new number. Remember to tell all of your contacts that you have changed your number. Have a good rest of your night. Glad I was able to help you. Is there anything else I can do for you?"

The lights in the store started turning off. It was time to go home.

"No ma'am. Thank you very much. You have been most helpful."

I finished signing the papers and Angela and I were off.

"I had no idea you could pick your own number, how did you know that? How did you know you could pick your own number? I have never seen anyone pick their own number. If I had known I could do that, I would have a number I could remember."

"If she can pick a number, there had to be a list she was looking at. I can pick one as easily as she can. You have to be brave girl!" I started to laugh. I knew why everyone can't pick their numbers, can you imagine how long that would take? Makes sense to just give them a number and say this is it.

Well about a week or so later, I had a voicemail on my phone from a number that I did not recognize. The message said:

"Uncle Jim is dying, if you want to see him, you need to come home."

I sat there and looked at my phone. Obviously this was important. I had no idea who Uncle Jim was, but the person who was supposed to hear the message didn't get it. That person wasn't given the choice to go home and see Uncle Jim one last time or not. Great. So, I called the number back. A woman answered because she recognized the number.

"I just listened to you message you left of my phone. I am so sorry to hear about your Uncle, I wish I could help, but I just got this number a week ago. I just wanted to let you know that whoever you were calling didn't get the message.

She started crying.

"I know loosing someone is difficult, even if you expect it. Is there anything I can do for you?"

"Yes, pray with me."

"Ok." I started to pray for her, her uncle, and her family.

"Thank you so much. That really helped me."

"I'm glad and I hope you get in touch with all of your family members in time."

We hung up and I decided that she must have been the reason that the number jumped out at me.

I heard God laughing. Hummm

The next night, I had just put my supper on the table when my phone rang. I answered it and heard a woman crying uncontrollably.

"Ok, calm down, how can I help you?" I recognized the woman's voice from the night before and I assumed Uncle Jim had passed.

"I am the woman you prayed with last night. I didn't know who else to call. I hope this is ok."

"Yes honey, it is ok. I recognized your voice, has Uncle Jim passed?"

"You sound white!"

"Yes, I am white, why? Does that make a difference to you?"

"I'm black!"

"Good, congratulations, now that that's out of the way, what's wrong?"

"My brother jumped off a six story building this morning! The hospital will not tell me anything about his condition, except that he's in ICU, critical and not expected to make it through the night."

Since she had a 504 number, I assumed she was in New Orleans.

"OK look, tell me where you are and I will come and get you

and we will go to the hospital and see about your brother. How does that sound?"

"I live in South Carolina and my sister KiKi, whose number you have lives in Texas!"

"Oh well, I live in New Orleans, so I guess I am not coming to get you in South Carolina."

"My brother is in New Orleans."

"Ok what hospital, I will go there and find out what his condition is and call you back."

"He's at University, but you can't go there this late, it's 8:30 at night"

"What is his name?"

"Marvin Johnson."

"What's your name?"

"Rose."

"OK, Rose, I will call you when I leave the hospital, where is it located?"

"Off Poydras, actually the street behind Poydras. Please, please, park under a street light. I don't want you hurt."

"I will be just fine Rose, promise."

I put on some shoes and headed out the door. I started praying that I could find out some useful information for her. I got to the hospital and went inside. When I walked up to the desk and asked for Marvin Johnsons room number, the black woman looked me up and down. (I am 5'7", short blonde hair and green eyes)

"Well, I got two Marvin Johnsons, which one do you want?"

I looked at her in disbelief, and said "Well, I bet, you don't have two that jumped off a six story building today do ya?"

"Who are you?"

"I am a friend of the family."

"Give me his birthday"

"Geeze, Almighty GD, really? Let me call his sister, hold on." I pulled out my phone and called Rose. "I am at the hospital. First she said she had two Marvin Johnson's and now she wants his birthday.

She doesn't believe I am a friend of the family. So Rose what is his birthday please?"

Before Rose could finish, the woman behind the desk said "He is on the second floor, in ICU, he's not expected to make it through the night, go on up."

I hung up with Rose and walked to the elevator and went to the second floor. Immediately stepping off the elevator was a sign. It was about 3'x4' and said in black bold letters "CHECK IN WITH THE POLICE OFFICERS BEFORE GOING ONTO THE FLOOR"

Great! What have I gotten into? I went looking for the police officers and found the two of them, sitting together, behind a table. "I want to see Marvin Johnson, please"

They looked me up and down. I was beginning to wonder if I was properly dressed! The black officer said "Who are you?"

"A friend of the family."

"Umm Humm, well his family is right over there in that waiting room, why don't you go be friendly." And he chuckled.

"I will do just that. Thank you for being so helpful!"

As I walked over to the waiting room, I was praying that GD would prepare their ears for me and give me the words to say to them. When I opened the door, directly in front of me and off to the left was a group of people that quite honestly, if they had guns, I would have been dead! YIKES! To the right, was another group of people, I was praying these were Marvin's people, they were not hostile looking. I walked over "Are you all Marvin's family?"

One tall elegant woman walked over. I assumed the family matriarch.

"Yes, Why? Who are you?"

"I am a friend of Rose and she has been trying to call you all, and can't get anyone, and the hospital will not tell her anything. She is really worried sick and I told her, that I would come and see what I could find out for her." Then I smiled.

"You been talking to her?"

"Yes, ma'am I have"

"You talked to her here at the hospital?"

"No, that would be difficult, she is in South Carolina." "I talked to her on the phone."

"Can you call her now on your phone and let me talk to her?"

"Yes, ma'am, I sure can."

I called Rose. "Rose I am at the hospital and your family is here. There is a lady here that wants to talk to you." I handed the matriarch my phone.

She walked to the back of the room. I just stood there. Well that was easy when she get back I can go home. I smiled to myself and again heard GD laughing. I sat down across from some more of Marvin's family and they started talking to me.

"Are you a pastor?"

"Uhh, no."

"OHHHH, but you preach right?"

"No, I'm Jewish, I don't preach."

Then at the top of her lungs this little woman I had been talking to screamed.

"Sweet Jesus, GD done sent us a Jew to pray with us, DAMN!"

They all gathered around. I couldn't figure out why everyone wanted me to pray with them. But pray I did for Marvin, his family gathered here and his family that is not here. When I finished. I was about to sit down and started explaining about Kiki's phone number.

"Oh, you know KiKi?"

"No, I don't know KiKi."

"You much better off girl. She's trouble."

They were trying to make sense of why a white woman was at University hospital in the middle of the night alone. It just didn't make sense to them.

"I just have her old number."

"Well, you have come all this way, would you like to go see him?"

Honestly, no that was the last thing I wanted to do. I just wanted to get my phone and go home. But then the Whisperers said "That is why you are here Sparkie" When I heard that my knees got weak. I looked at the woman talking to me.

"Yes, I would like to see him."

"We can't believe you came here, this will be the last time you will ever see him, cause he's dying tonight, they killed him and are going to get away with that too."

"Wait who killed him, I thought he jumped off a six story building."

"Naw, they throwed him off the building."

"Who threw him off what building?"

We had been talking as we were winding through the halls.

"There he is."

I looked up and nearly fainted. There was a young man lying in a hospital bed that was hooked up to every kind of machine you could imagine! I had never seen so many machines, most of them I didn't recognize. There was every type of tube coming out of him that you could possibly imagine. His right hand was closest to me and his fingers were curved around, not tight but like they were waiting for something to be put in them. I put two of my fingers in his right hand and closed my eyes. I started sending white light through his body, concentrating on the part of his body that I could see were damaged. After a few minutes, I felt a smack on my left shoulder. I opened my eyes and turned to see a little blonde haired, blue eyed nurse all in white standing there.

"Yes?"

"Don't wake him up, we had to give him pain medication about an hour ago, he's not going to make it."

"Wait, what? Wait a minute, he has been here all day long in pain and you just gave him pain medication an hour ago?"

"Yes, we were not sure he was in pain."

"Are you kidding me? Honey I teach art and I have enough sense to know if you fall off a six story building you are going to be in pain. I will bet you, that if your happy ass fell off a six story building, you would have gotten pain medication a long time ago!"

"Exactly, who are you?"

"I am a friend of the family. Who are you?"

"I am Mr. Johnson's nurse."

"Umm Humm, don't you have to take an oath about helping people. Not watching them be in pain?"

"Well take a good look friend of the family, because he is not going to make it through the night."

"Well Mr. Johnson's nurse. You take a good look at him because he is not dying on my watch and he's going to live a long time. Now go away and let me finish."

She turned and walked away. The woman who came in with me now had her back to me snickering. She turned and looked at me, held my arm. "Thank you for standing up for Marvin. Nobody ever did that. Thank you for whatever you can do for him."

"Well, GD isn't finished with him yet and he is going to be fine. You can believe that."

I finished sending white light and fixing what I saw wrong with him and we went back to the waiting room. Rose's aunt was still on the phone with Rose. She ended the conversation and walked up gave me a hug and handed me the phone. I headed out of the waiting room. The officers nodded as I left.

"Good evening Officers."

When I got into my car I called Rose.

"Thank you so much for going, I am sorry it was a waste of time. He ain't gonna make it Sparkie."

"You're wrong Rose, he is going to be just fine."

"I can't believe that. They are saying he isn't even going to make it through the night. He can't breathe on his own, he is awful broke up."

Yes, he was broken up. I saw lots of broken bones and bruised muscles. I had worked on him for over an hour. I had no idea how long it was but according to my car clock I had been gone 2.5 hours!

"Do you believe GD can heal?'

"Yes."

"Then believe he is going to be fine, because he is."

"My family has my number now, so they will keep me posted on Marvin. You don't have to go back."

"Ok, but keep me posted on him as well please. Will ya?"

"Sure."

We said goodnight and I drove home to River Ridge.

The next morning my phone rang. It was Rose.

"Hello Rose, how is Marvin?"

Sparkie, they took his breathing tube out today! Do you believe that?"

"Sure do. He will get better and better every day, promise. How's your Uncle?'

"No change. But he is not dead."

Several days after that my phone rang and it was again Rose.

"Hay, how's Marvin doing Rose?"

"He is better; he has started writing notes now. He wants me to come visit. I don't have the money to get there. I was wondering if you could help with that? I just need a ticket on the bus to get me there. I can stay with family and friends and I have enough money to get back on."

"I don't have that much money, but let me see what I can do and I will call you back."

"Ok, I will talk to you later."

We hung up. I had no idea where I was going to get the money. I asked a Pastor who was one of the parents of the school I was teaching in. I told him the story and he looked at me. "No, tell her to ask each of her friends and family to give her $20.00 and she will soon have it." I couldn't believe my ears! I just stood there dumb founded. Then the Whisperers said, 'Rabbi Lowey'. So I went into see my Rabbi. I told him the same story and without hesitation, my synagogue, Gates of Prayer, gave me a check to help a woman they never met to be able to come and see her brother. I have never been so proud to be a part of anything as I was that day.

I got to see her face to face. What an adventure this had become, and from something so small as picking my own 504 number!

Marvin last I heard was living in South Carolina with his sister Rose.

I share this story to tell you to trust your feelings, because the smallest thing could turn out to be something very large and important in the grand scheme of things. As my friend Shaman John says, we just need to show up, the universe will do the rest.

Annie

I started dating an old acquaintance from college in 2013. We not only lived in different towns, we lived in different states! The long distance relationship was kept alive by frequent phone calls and text messages. I was invited to come to Bowling Green, Kentucky for a visit, and stay at his house. I accepted. It was a long 8.5-hour drive from New Orleans, but I had my dogs with me and it didn't bother me. I listened to the radio and sang all the way there.

His home was a beautiful large place with a log addition, the upstairs was added by Bob. When I pulled into the driveway, I got the feeling of abandonment. Odd. He came out to greet me and I asked "What is her name?" Exasperated he said, "Good Lord, you name houses too?" "well, she's wooden and rock, so she has to be alive and have a name." His look of bewilderment told me to just keep this to myself. "Never mind, I'll let you know when she tells me." He just looked at me and nodded taking in a deep breath. I knew this was going to be an interesting stay.

We walked into the house from the back door, through his pottery studio and into the kitchen area. I couldn't believe my eyes. "Oh my God, you're a horder?"

"No, I am not." Looking around there was a path through the kitchen winding up the staircase to the master bedroom. That should have been enough of a red flag to run back to New Orleans, but it wasn't.

The next morning, Bob went to the gallery and I stayed at the house. I wanted to start cleaning up. Good grief! It wasn't long before I heard "Annie, my name is Annie." I was in the living room, making a path of sorts. I stopped and said "Wait, what?" It was almost a whisper.

"My name is Annie, you asked what my name was, it's Annie". Oh WOW, the Spirit was talking to me. I was so excited to hear her.

"Hi Annie, my name is Sparkie. It's a pleasure to meet you."

"I can't believe you are starting to clean up here."

"Yeah, me either. I have no idea where to start. You are so beautiful! You just can't be seen. Wow!"

"Thank you for doing this. I thought I would just die and no one would even notice. It's been 11 years since anyone noticed me. He just uses me as a storage place, a place to sleep, grab coffee and leave. He is never here."

"Well I am just visiting, but I thought I would start doing some laundry." There was a wheel barrel in the short path in the living room full of dirty clothes that had been thrown over the banister. Then I walked toward the laundry room. Clothes were knee deep; I am not exaggerating. I started to make my way into the laundry room and the pile was up to my thigh. So I started laundry. I looked around at what could be done and probably not noticed. I found out very quickly that Annie had an agenda of her own. I could feel and hear her telling me what she wanted accomplished. Some of the things were way too complicated and would take hours. When I started to do what I thought would take a short 15 minutes or so, if it wasn't on her agenda, it was like herding cats. There was no end to it. When I went along with her, a job that would have taken maybe an hour or better, took right at 15 minutes! So, we reached a mutual agreement, we did it her way. I got smart and started having conversations with her. "So, Annie, what do you want done next?"

Meanwhile, Bob was at the pottery studio, where I had first run into him again. He was working and I was playing with Annie. Both of us were getting a lot done. When he came home, I was excited. "Hi, I found out her name." "Hiii, whose name?" "Your house's name. It's Annie." "Annie? Whose Annie? What?" He just shook his head and grinned at me, like I was crazy. I could tell he didn't believe me and this was a dead end. So, I took another route.

"Annie, Bob doesn't believe you are real. Could you somehow show him how real you are?" I didn't get a verbal answer, but I did get the feeling the next few hours were going to be interesting.

That night, he got up to go to the bathroom. He came storming back to the bedroom and started screaming.

"Sparkie! How the hell did you lock that door?" I woke up, trying to make sense of what he was saying. "What door? What are you screaming about?"

"The door to the hallway. Hell, I built this place and I didn't know it would lock!"

I started walking with him out of the bedroom. At the top of the staircase there is a landing. If you go to the right and through a door, you will go to the two bathrooms on the left and two bedrooms on the right. When he was married, the boy's rooms were down that hallway. If you go the left, you will go up two steps and to the landing in front of the master bedroom. Looking to the left, you will be overlooking living room. It has a beautiful stone fireplace that is fit for a castle. It is huge. (I always figured that if a tornado came I would be in the fireplace with room left over.) Bob brought petrified wood and stones from all over the United States to be part of the fireplace. He hand built it and it is a thing of beauty. When we had fires in it at night, and then went to bed; the glow could still be seen from the fire in the bedroom. He uses the fireplace to heat the house with in the winter. That doesn't work so very well. There are bookcases on the walls perpendicular to it. Just a beautiful room. The master bedroom to the left has double doors. I always wanted to see French doors there. As you come into the room there are two walk in closets on either side.

We walked to the top of the landing. The door was shut. I never really noticed it before. I stood there puzzled until I hear Annie laughing. OH, ok. "Bob, I know you are going to find this hard to believe, but I didn't lock the door. I never really noticed it before. Actually, Annie locked it. See I asked her if she would show you she was real since you didn't believe me. This is Annie showing you she's real."

He looked at me perplexed and tried the door again. It was locked and not opening.

"You know you could ask her to open it."

He just stood there nodding his head up and down. "Annie this isn't funny, he now knows you are real, will you please open the door." At that instant, the door handle popped and the door swung open about 12 inches. I just grinned, then I heard Bob say.

"All I wanted to do was go pee." And he walked down the hallway. Annie was still laughing. "Thank you, that was impressive." I went back to bed laughing. Annie had just made him a believer!

She was very happy now with her rooms starting to be cleaned and her house looking like a home again. To prove to her he believed she was real, he made a necklace for her from Kentucky red stone. It hung above the doorway going from the living room to the main hallway. I am no longer with Bob and so I don't know how Annie is doing now, but my prayer is that she is just fine and happy.

<.......>

My Sister Sherry

In February of 2013, my phone rang. "Hay sis, I was thinking of coming down for Fat Tuesday, would that be ok?"

"No! Come down the Wednesday before. We will party and hit all of the parades. Fat Tuesday is just for tourists. We have been parting since 12th night and some of the best parades are the week before. Come down, I will pick you up at the airport and I will pay for everything. How does that sound?"

"Let me see what I can work out, I will call you back. That's less than a week away."

I got a call that night and she had cleared her calendar, she was an insurance salesperson in Arkansas. I picked her up at the airport and we went to my apartment in River Ridge, a small community on the outskirts of New Orleans. We dropped her bags, and headed out. That began the week of frivolity in the last Mardi Gras Festival she would ever be at.

This was the first time that we had ever spent time alone together since we were kids. No husbands, no kids. It proved to be a magical time for us. We became very close, old wounds forgotten, and merely becoming friends. After that time together, we talked on the phone daily, sometimes 3-4 times a day, sharing, and catching up, giving words of encouragement, laughing together, it was a fantastic time.

In May, she and her husband Lex, were rear ended by a battery truck as they sat at a stop light. She hit her head on the left hand side as it collided with the window. Sherry started having headaches. She had never before had a problem with them. This worried me and I stayed on her till she went to see the doctor. He said they found a spot on her brain, a bruise if you will. He said it was caused by her being sent forwarded with such force. The bruise turned into a small tumor. Nothing to worry about, until her balance became difficult for her to walk. Her speech became slurred, and I became worried. I knew something was horribly wrong. I tried to get her to come down here and see some real doctors, but she was sure her doctor was good. I was sure of the opposite! Her doctor told her the tumor was slightly larger and that was causing all the trouble, nothing to worry about!

"Sherry, please come down here, I will pay for you to see the doctors here. They are some of the best in the world. Something is desperately wrong with you. I will pay for it, just come. I can come up and get you and bring you down here, please."

"No, I'm fine."

This was in September. By October my daughter Sarah called. "Mama, aunt Sherry is in Hospice." "What? Hospice? How can that be?" I hung up and called. Lex answered, I rarely got to speak to her now.

"Really she is fine, I just needed some help with her."

"OMG, no Lex." When New Orleans Hospice is called, it is to help the person transition from this world to the next. I took off from school that Thursday and drove to Mountain Home, Arkansas. I arrived in the wee hours of the morning. I crashed on the couch. On Friday morning, when I heard them up, I got up and went to see my sister. I was shocked! I hardly recognized her. She was bed fast, her face was bruised and swollen, supposedly from her last fall. I just couldn't believe my eyes! She smiled and patted the bed beside her. I sat down, gave her a hug and fought not to fall apart.

She would start to talk, get frustrated and wanting me to talk for her. I would make her use her words. We laughed together that day. I told her stories of my students and of Bob, the man I was dating. We enjoyed our time together. When I helped her change her diapers, I noticed bed sores. I applied medication to them. While she napped I had a meeting with Lex. He and I had spoken weekly and he had never told me of her condition or that she had bed sores. He was in denial that she was dying. My sister was dying and neither her husband or myself wanted to see it.

On Saturday, Sherry was more talkative than the day before. She pointed to the closet.

"Get it."

"Get what, use your words Sis."

"Ummm, in closet, picture in envelop, Get It Out."

"Ok." I went to the closet, on the right hand side, in the back was a large envelope used to transport prints in. I pulled it out.

"Yes!" she squealed. "That's it. Daddy gave this to me in 1972 and told me to keep it. I am supposed to give it to you when the time is right. It's time."

I pulled out the prints one at a time. The first one was of the capital building in Frankfort, KY. She shook her head no. When I pulled out the second one, I was looking at a very familiar face, a kind, and wise face. I knew that face!

"That one. Tell me stories."

"I don't know what to tell you honey. I have known him since I was a little girl and you went to school. I haven't seen him in years! He was always with me then. He and my arch angel. I think he is one of the Whisperers that talk to me now. I cannot believe you have had him so very long."

"Take him with you."

"Gladly!"

"Can you put white light in me?"

"Of course I can."

"Do it now please."

So I scooted over to her and closed my eyes. I asked for myself to be pure enough to let this healing work be done. I prayed for assistance from my Spirit Helpers, Arc Angels, The All Father, and the Holy Spirit. This was before I knew Snake was my healing Spirit.

"Close your eyes baby."

She did and I laid my hands on the sides of her head. The instant I put my hands on her head I could feel the power going into her body. I started at her head and worked my way through her body mentally naming her organs and asking for healing. When I got to her heart a strange thing happened. The Whisperers said "This is where she needs healing. Stay here." So I did. I stayed at her heart for a long time. I couldn't see what was happening or what was wrong, but I could feel the energy go into that area and a lot of it. I was very new at healing when this was going on. I didn't know to make myself a hollow bone and have the energy used run through me. I only knew that the energy would leave me and heal people. I always felt tired afterwards. But this time I felt like I had run a 10K marathon. I was totally drained, so much so I had to end our session. I know now to open myself up to let the energy flow through me and into the person I am working on, not to use my own energy. I gave thanks for all of the help I received during the healing of my sister. She was peacefully sleeping now with a smile on her glowing face. That was a first for me as well, the glowing. I laid down beside her and kept my hand on her. We slept for several hours together. Lex came in with dinner. We ate together. I got her ready for bed, gave her medicine and called it a night.

The next morning, I was up early, not looking forward to the nine-hour drive home. I went into her room and she grabbed my hand.

"I will see you Thanksgiving, promise."

A tear slipped from her eye. "Thank you."

"For what? I will be back Thanksgiving, we are off a whole week and we can visit longer. By then you will have had your chemo and be back on your feet." My experience with healing was physical, like Melvin. They get better and live their lives like normal. That was what I was expecting.

"For the healing, I feel wonderful, it's wonderful. I'm not scared now." Even as she said this, tears were flowing down both of our faces.

"Stop crying. I will see you in a couple of weeks. Wait, I will come for your birthday on the second! How about that? That's closer, is that ok?"

She just nodded her head yes, but the tears didn't stop and the look in her eyes said everything. I left her crying and drove the next hour crying. I knew what she was saying and I didn't want to hear it. That was one of the hardest things I have ever done in my life, just to leave her crying, knowing that I would never see her alive again, but I didn't have any more days to be able to take off and I had to go back.

I got a call on October 21st from my daughter Sarah. I was already at school. "Mama, Aunt Sherry is at Hospice House. They don't think she is going to make it another day, maybe two. If you want to see her, you need to get up here now."

I went to my principal and told her. I left right after lunch. I went home packed a bag and got Sargent Major. We headed to Mountain Home. I got there early Tuesday morning. I went to Sherry's house and got directions to Hospice House. Lex and I went to see Sherry. I could tell she had already started to transition. I gave her a kiss on her forehead and I sat down in the chair beside her bed, holding her hand. I knew for certain then why she was crying when I left her. She knew she wouldn't make it to Thanksgiving. As I sat there I started thinking about the healing she said she could feel, obviously, it wasn't a physical healing. Later that night Sarah and her friend arrived. I was settled into one of the chairs in the Hospice House room when they came in. It was a nice, clean, quiet place. Sherry had been unresponsive but I held her hand and talked to her anyway. Morning broke. Sarah, Lex and Karen came in. Later that morning, I saw the doctor. "Excuse me, what is your best guess as to how long my sister will be with us?" He looked at me questioningly. "I want the truth, don't blow sunshine."

"Are all of her family here that are coming?" "Yes." "She has been waiting for everyone. I would say a day maybe two, but not more than that."

"Ok, thank you."

All of a sudden Karen got upset, it was her daughter's birthday and she didn't want Sherry to die on that day. "I will talk to her and she will wait till tomorrow."

"Can you do that? Thank you. I love her or I wouldn't be here. My baby will have plenty of birthday's but I wanted to tell Sherry good-bye, she was so good to me."

I leaned over the bed and spoke in my sister's ear. "Today is Karen's daughter's birthday. She would appreciate it if you could hold out till after midnight. Would that be ok?' She smiled.

Sarah and I stayed with her all night, each of us holding a hand on the opposite sides of the bed. At midnight I leaned over. "Thank you Sissy, you can go home now sweetie, give Daddy a hug and kiss from me." She left before daybreak. Sarah looked at me.

"Mama, I think she is gone."

Yes, she was. I went to get the nurse and Lex if he was here. Lex walked in looked at her and left. I thought at the time that was very cold. But everyone walks this path differently. Sarah and I stayed with her till the funeral home came and got her. The nurse on the floor stopped by and asked me how I knew she was not going till after midnight. She and I had had that conversation in the hallway earlier the day before.

"Because I asked her not to leave till after midnight, and I told her when midnight was, so she could transition."

She's been gone for seven years now and I still miss her. I have things to show her and talk to her about. It just doesn't seem possible. So, if you have a loved one that you have spent most of your life not talking to or visiting with. Life is short and quirky, build that bridge!! You will not regret it.

Jerry Foxworth

On Wednesday, January 29th, 2014, we were out of school for ice. It was our second day to be closed for ice! The only thing unusual about it was, I was living in New Orleans, Louisiana! We rarely get ice and snow, so it was very unusual.

My phone rang. "Sparkie?" "I just wanted to let you know that Jerry passed." "No, when I just talked to her, she was making chicken noodle soup. She can't be gone!" "Sparks, you gonna be ok?" I just nodded. I couldn't breathe, much else answer the question. I was sitting on the side of my bed. Sargent Major, my westie, jumped up on the bed beside me and got into my lap. He always knew when something was wrong. My heart hurt!! One of my dearest friends and mentors had just passed. I couldn't believe it. I started reliving all the times we had together. I put my phone down. Tears were running down my face. Then I heard her voice! My first thought was, I am making this up because I want to hear her! But in saying that out loud, I knew my voice and that wasn't what I was hearing! I heard Jerry talking to me! I love her so.

"No, Sparks, it's me! I'm fine, I can dance! I am happy, please don't worry about me girl. I'm not in pain any more. Now you go on!" She giggled and was gone. What you need to know about Miss Jerry is that she was overweight, and had a hard time walking. She taught pre-K at Morris Jeff Community School when I met her. Such an inspiration! She was a strong woman and I miss her. She would always tell me "Now you go on!"

I just sat on my bed processing what had just happened. Granted, I miss her a great deal, but I know she is happy and dancing and thought enough of me to reassure me that she was fine, she was that kind of friend and woman.

"Now you go on!" How appropriate that was. Jerry giving me the forward order to get off my duff and get back to work!

At her memorial service we were told she was a solider, who fought for her students. We were also told we needed to carry on. She was a lightworker in every meaning of the word. I had already been given my direct order to carry on! I only hope that I am the example that she was to me!

While typing Jerry's story up Jerry decided to visit me! I didn't pick this font, she did!! It's June 21, 2020. 10 o'clock on a Sunday night. I had gotten to the part of the story that says:

"No, Spark's, it's me."

Then the computer froze, kinda. The mouse would work anywhere I wanted to put it but, I could not move the document or anything on the document. I pulled up other stories no problem, go to Jerry's story and nothing. Couldn't type on it or move it up or down! I couldn't figure out how to fix it. I turned the computer off. Turning it back on did not help. Still nothing.

I then told her that if she didn't want this story in the book to let me know. I would start this story again if the same thing happened, I would leave it out. So I started the same story on a clean sheet. I couldn't remember what I had typed. I was going back and forth from the first one to the second one. Then the screen went crazy. And the first one disappeared and a white sheet with a red line across the top showed up and the letters us.

I deleted that sheet then a plain white one showed up. I deleted that one as well then I was back to the second paper and saved it as jerry foxworth.

When I opened up all of the documents in word only the jerry foxworth document showed up but at the bottom was recover unsaved documents. I hit it and the first jerry foxworth document showed up but in a split page. Part of it on the left side and the rest on the right side. The mouse was effective on this paper so I started to copy it. I copied the left side went to the second paper and pasted it on to it. When I went back to the first paper it was normal not a split page. It is the one I am typing on now. So I guess Jerry is still here. I miss you girl!

April 6ᵗʰ, 2014

Becoming Aware of Something New

I awakened Sunday morning with a very vivid dream in my mind. I had been at a church service with my Grandmother. I wondered why she was there since she passed a long time before this, but then there was a deceased friend there as well. Odd, Jerry didn't know Grandmother but they appear to be old friends! When the service was over, I was headed to Fellowship Hall, but I ended up in a market place that seemed to be part of the church! They were selling odd things for a church; like jewelry, and pottery. I kept looking for someone I knew. I couldn't find Bob, my husband at the time.

So I got into my car and I drove to a home that I was familiar with. I know no one was home, but I also knew it was ok for me to go inside. It was homey. I went onto the long, narrow screened in porch. Sitting on a green and white stripped couch, was a special needs little girl. She was trying to eat something out of a white enamel bucket. The top of the bucket had rust on it where the enamel hade chipped off. Around the bottom and some places on the sides were rusted. On the outside of the bucket was a note that read, "Eat this, they are figs." I looked in the bucket to see it was full of shells, pebbles, and dirt! Some mud was in there as well. The little girl had reddish brown hair, cut in a bob. She had dirt on her hands and face, she had been trying to eat the shells in the bucket! I took the bucket away from her. "Honey, these are not figs, you shouldn't eat them. These are shells and rocks and mud." I put the bucket where she couldn't get it.

I left her and went inside the house to the living room. I sat down on a rough brown couch. I had my sketch pad in my hand and a long, heavy gray trench coat that I had just taken off, over my arm. Across from the couch was a picture window that looked out onto a large meadow. Very pretty! I left my coat and sketch pad on the couch and went into the bathroom. As I opened the door and tried to walk in, it was very small, I noticed that the toilet was on the right with the bathtub across from it and the sink was right next to the toilet. I lifted the seat cover and there was muddy water with yellow things floating in it, I closed the lid. When I turned around to face the bath tub, there was some of the same water in one corner of the tub. The bathroom was spotless except for the muddy water! There was no smell. I looked out the window and saw parked in front of my car, on the single lane grassy road, were three more cars that were not there when I came. I headed outside, thinking that I might find someone. At the screen door, I remembered my sketch pad and my coat. I stopped and started to turn around when a really cool, strong wind blew from behind me. It pushed me out the door. My skirt blew toward the door and the Whisperers told me "Leave them, she can have them, you don't need them anymore."

I headed outside to my car. My car looked the same on the outside, but when I looked in the driver's door, there were no seats, steering wheel or anything that remotely resembled the inside of my car as I knew it. The back of my Kia was filled with plats of seedlings! What was going on??! I looked up and a tall skinny man in overalls with a light tee shirt on under them was heading my way. I was leaning with my head against the roof of the Kia, almost in tears!

"Ain't that always the way. People come by in the afternoon and all they want is money!"

"No, I don't need money, I need to know what's going on!"

"Mornins just like afternoon. Days just like afternoons."

I woke up sort of. You know when you're waking up but you are still in that in between stage, not awake and not asleep? That's where I was, not asleep, but definitely not awake! Bob was already up, so I got up, but I did not wake up. I walked into things, fell over things, dropped the coffee basket, spilling coffee all over the coffee maker and counter and floor! I could not connect with the world I was in, I was just a couple of seconds off, which doesn't sound like a lot but it really is major! I stumbled into the living room and grabbed my dream notebook. I wrote the dream down. When I finished writing it down, I was completely awake! Wide awake!

I thought about this off and on all day long. I didn't quite understand the whole process or what it meant. This was a first for me, to be walking around not awake but definitely not asleep. It was truly strange. When we got back from work, I knew I needed a nap. Bob listened as I laid out everything that happened. "I'm sorry you didn't sleep well." "It wasn't that I didn't sleep well, I couldn't wake up! All I want to know is what is going on?" At that exact moment I knew! The Whisperers told me.

"You were your car. Your outsides will look the same, but your insides are changing and the change will be forever. You will be helping people and planting seeds of knowledge, hope, and wisdom in the parts of the world where people feel like they are the toilet of the world."

How amazing!! How exciting! I was sure these half-awake time will become more frequent. But for now I know to immediately write them down and to ponder upon them. The answer will always come.

I no longer live in Bowling Green and Bob is no longer in my life. I have certainly changed from where I was in 2014. It's now 2020. I no longer teach art; I have been teaching English as a Second Language to students who are refugees from other countries for two years now. I teach junior high school, 6,7,8ᵗʰ grades. These students have become my family and I love each and every one of them. I live in Treme in New Orleans, I do not need a heavy trench coat. Even the winters here are not cold.

Always pay attention to your dreams. What they show you doesn't always come immediately, which is why you need to keep a dream journal and sometimes on a rainy day read some of your dreams. When you can discern a pattern, then you will know when your Whisperers are talking to you. Their message to you may be about future events. Be brave, you can always ask what is going on, what does this mean! It could mean lots of wonderful things!

Quantum Jumping

And Snake

I had taken a course on quantum jumping through Mindvalley. com. It is a way to lift your vibrations to be where you want to be. While meditating, you "quantum jump" to the vision you have of yourself and where you want to be. Once you can hold onto those vibrations, you can achieve that goal.

I was living in Kentucky in a situation that was not very copacetic. I meditated daily, usually listening to drumming and journeying. I was in the living room of the log house, whose Spirit was named Anne. Sitting on the leather couch, looking around at the huge stone fireplace, I was grateful for being alive and being able to sit here among these old stones and petrified wood. The stones came from all over the United States. The opening was large enough for two people to sit comfortably in. I always thought that if a tornado came, I would stay in the fireplace. A peace fell over me as I was contemplating what to do. This particular day, I could not find my headphones, so instead of journeying, I decided to try quantum jumping.

I first quantum jumped into the financially independent me.

She was at the kitchen table at 525 Madison Street in New Orleans, LA., drinking coffee and going over the ending of the cold storage list. The coffee smelled great and there was a breeze coming in from the patio across the dining room. There was the smell of rain in the air. A beautiful day. I caught the vibration of her and felt that peace again all around me. Then the jump was over and I was back in KY.

That's when I decided to meditate without drumming. Snake came right up to me! I was surprised to see him because I thought I only saw him I was doing a healing. "I have some healing on you that needs to be taken care of," he said. Then he wrapped around my shoulder, and went down my left leg, wrapping around it as he went. When he got to my foot, he took it in his mouth and bit it, sinking his fangs into my ankle. There was no pain. He wound back up my left leg and crossed over to my right leg. He did exactly the same thing to it, wound around it and coming to my foot took it into his mouth and bit it, sinking his fangs into my right ankle. Then he wound around my right leg as he went back up my leg. At my hip he started to wrap around my torso, I felt a great sadness leaving me. Then he took my heart in his mouth and bit it, sinking his fangs into it, tears of relief ran down my cheeks. The procedure was the same for my arms. Wounding around them and when he got to my hands he would place them in his mouth and bit them, sinking his fangs into my wrists. He then looked at me "You are mine, I am your power, I am going to consume you." With his body wrapped around my torso, he opened his mouth, dislodging his jaw and put my head into it. He swallowed my entire body, unwrapping me as he went. At my feet he turned and did the same thing. When he got finished, he laid his head next to mine resting on my right shoulder, his body resting, draped across my left shoulder and down my arm, with most of his magnificent body lying in my lap.

I had the strangest thought. In a book I had read, this kind of thing happened to the hearo, who was a Native American. Only with him it was a horned, winged underwater serpent, and he grabbed the horn, breaking off a piece. They were not friends, but enemies.

The hero won the fight, he kept the piece of the horn to prove he had won. I didn't need proof I was one with snake. Healings and time would definitely tell that by itself.

As if reading my thoughts, snake looked at me, "You need no proof." then he was gone.

I have often thought of this meditation since it happened. Thinking of it brings tears to my eyes and I feel any sadness leave me. It was a weight of some kind. I am sure if it was important enough for me to know what it was that was removed, I would have been told. I am grateful it was removed and that Snake and I do healings together even today.

A Past Life Revealed

3/15/15

I had been up extremely late the night before celebrating my daughter Sarah's birthday. I had not slept well that night either. So this afternoon, I had laid down for a quick nap. I immediately went into a deep sleep. I had a Vision!

I was wearing a long dress and my hair was in done in shoulder length curls. The type you see in an old tin type, photos taken before, during and after the Civil War. I believe the time was earlier or long after the war. I was hearing this beautiful song in the background of this Vision. I started to hum it. We were decorating for Christmas! The smell of cooking was coming from the kitchen and decorations were being hung. The house was a very busy place. It was glorious! As I walked through the house, I realized it was the exact same floor plan as Annie, the place where I was living at the time!

I walked to the balcony and looked over. There was a huge Christmas tree in the corner by the fireplace. A fire in the fireplace and holly and evergreens are strung everywhere. I turned around and opened the French doors to our bedroom. On the night stand, I saw pictures of me and Bob. He was dressed as a Union officer. I had on a white wedding gown. One of the pictures was very formal, no smile not cutting up none of that. The other three were of him horsing around with me. He was thrown across my lap and acting like his silly self! We looked so happy!

All the while the song was playing in the background. I started singing the words to it as I walked through the house, enjoying everything I saw. I went down the stairs and out onto the front porch. It was painted and decorated and just lovely. I went down the stairs to the walkway through the front yard. The yard was much, much bigger. It had a place for carriages to circle in front of the porch and to come to the back of the house where the barn was as well. At the end of the walk, there was a round arch made of stone.

Putting up garland on the top of this stone archway, was a black man dressed in a waist coat. He was on some sort of ladder. The Whisperers said "He is not a slave; he is a happy worker for you." I guess I was wondering about that. I went up to him and smiled, he was smiling at me and he took his hands and cupped them and then blew across them. What came out looked like "Fairy Dust" for lack of a better description. It was fine and iridescent, shimmering in the light. It was extraordinary! He blew this at me and he was laughing, a deep belly laugh as he was doing it. I felt like I was in a snow globe. It was one of the most magical thing I had ever experienced! I was filled with love and joy and peace. They were all around me, consuming me into them. It's difficult to explain how this felt. I woke up humming the tune. But since that time, I have not been able to hum it or sing it.

During the Christmas Holidays in 2014, I had gone out shopping and was led to a second hand bookstore. I looked in the metaphysical section and didn't see anything that caught my attention, but I knew there was something there that I was supposed to have. I saw a Dr. Wayne Dyer book with a cd and I bought it. I left knowing that I didn't get what I was sent after. Later that night Bob and I were going to a movie, we had some time to kill and ended up in the same bookstore I was in earlier that day. I went to the Jewish section this time and I saw a book that was called "Study of the Sacred Wheel". I thought it was about the medicine wheel, so I gladly bought it. And added it to my collection of worthy books. We went to the movie and headed home. I didn't get a chance to look at my new find that night, but the next morning over coffee, I opened it up to discover that it was a workbook on Shamanism. My mouth fell open! I had been praying about whether to go to study under Valery Nunley or go to New Mexico to study at the Shaman School there. I knew it was time for me to get busy doing something. I told Bob while I was laughing what the book was about. "I told you that you needed to get off your butt and do something." The workbook was wonderful. I looked up Lynn Andrews on Google. OMG! She was there. I went to her website and low and behold she had a school. I read about it and knew this was where I was supposed to be. I applied to the school and was accepted.

My first books came. I was so excited! I opened the box. There were books and CD's and a long letter. I pulled out a green book called Coming Full Circle. I opened it and started to read. On the second page was the song from my vision!! I read it and reread it! I couldn't believe it, I could hear the music and the song. I knew then that I had chosen the right place to go. Peace settled over me. I knew I was on my way on a magical path.

It is now 2020. My path has been so very interesting. It has taken twists and turns but always headed in the right direction. It is still magical.

Keeping a journal helps me see where I have been but more importantly, where I am going. It will do the same thing for you. Try it. Write what comes to your heart. Doesn't have to be long, doesn't have to be short. You just have to start it and the Universe will show up to do their part.

Krewe De Vieux

Carnival 2019! I am living in New Orleans and loving it! I had gone to Chewbacchus, a Star Wars Parade that was magnificent! But tonight was Krewe De Vieux, another one of my favorites. I was meeting Vicki and her family at Coop's Place on Decatur St. Since I live near the French Quarter, I decided I would walk there. It was just 8 blocks up and 4 blocks or so up Decatur. I got dressed for the evening in all black, my favorite color. I arrived at Coop's a little early. I stood on the street watching the costumed people parade by. Everyone was having a great time and the streets were clogged with people. There were a lot of blind referees that year, due to a very bad non call in the Saints last football game, that cost us a chance at the Championship. I had just made pictures of a husband and wife both dressed as blind referees when a man came across the crowded street and walked up to me and started talking. "Hi, I'm Ben from Boston." I smiled "Hi Ben from Boston, I'm Sparkie from New Orleans." "Oh my God you actually live here?" "Yes, there are a lot of us that live here, amazing isn't it." "So, Sparkie, are you alone?" "No, Ben I am not but thank you for asking." "Really? Because you look like you're alone." "Well, you know what they say, Looks' can be deceiving." "Yes, but I like the way you look." "Thank you again, but I really am with a group of people, they just haven't gotten here yet." "Oh, well, I'm eating at Coop's, want to join me?" "No, I am joining my friends, Ben. You probably need to go get in line. It looks like that line to get in is long." "No, see those men over there? The ones with the ties on?" "Yes." "I am with them and they are in line. So I can stay here and talk to you." "I am a lucky girl then aren't I?" "Well you could be later." "Umm, no I will not be taking you up on that. Oh look your people are going in, you need to go with them and get a seat, don't you think?" "I am not leaving you out here by yourself, someone may try to hurt you. I am staying with you till your group gets here." "Nope, you're not. See they are hollering for you. Go on really I will be fine." "Are you sure? I can wait." "Oh I am positive. Bye." Before Ben went inside, he handed me his card. "Here is my card, call me if you get into trouble." I took the card went inside asked the bartender for a pen, wrote my name and phone number on the card and went back outside to Ben. "Here is your card back, on the back is my name and number, call me if you get into trouble." He looked at me funny and started laughing, then Ben went inside. Shortly after Ben left, Vicki and the fam showed up. We didn't have to wait in line, we all went right to the bar and got a drink. As we were walking in, Ben got up and walked over, "Hi, you must be Vicki, Sparkie has told me so much about you, I am Ben from Boston and we are together tonight." "What are you talking about, Ben? We are not together; you are with the men at that table. Ben, go sit down and finish eating so you don't miss Krewe De Vieux Parade. It's really the best in Carnival." I got a strange look from Vicki that said, I want to hear this story.

Ben sat down to eat and we went upstairs. "So Sparks, you pick up someone while you were waiting?" "No, Vicki, he came up and started talking but no, he's drunk and with a group from his bank in Boston." "Well, I don't know, he's cute." "Yes, I agree but I don't need someone in Boston." The parade started and I was out of a beer, so I went back down to the bar. Ben was sitting finishing up supper. I walked over, "Ben you are missing the parade." He just nodded and I left.

I enjoyed the parade and walked home much to the disgruntled remarks of Vicki, who thought I might get mugged. "I walk these streets every Wednesday night to listen to Bill and The Tempted play at BMC. Promise I will be fine." "Text me when you get home." "No worries." And I headed home. It was a great night for a walk. I love New Orleans.

I texted Vicki when I got home and got my dog Daisy and we went for a walk. When we got home, she got a treat and I got ready for bed. It was 1:30 am. My phone rang;" Sparkie?" "Yes" "This is Ben from Boston, I was wondering if you wanted to have lunch or breakfast tomorrow?" "Sure Ben, call me when you get up and we will make plans then." We talked for a few minutes longer. It seems he had gotten caught up in the parade and walked in the parade for several blocks, till he got close to his hotel. He had long since lost his group of workers.

My phone rang at 8, it was Ben they had a business breakfast and he would call later. The weekend went like that, plans made and business took precedence over all, which it should have. He had invited me to the banquet on Sunday before they left on Monday. I declined. He called Monday when he got to the airport. We talked till his plane was called.

When Ben went back to Boston, we talked at night usually when he was in the car. I assume going to or from a meeting. One Wednesday night he called upset. He had been to the doctor and was told he had prostate cancer. They were doing a biopsy on Friday. "Ben, I am a healer, can I do some energy work on you tonight and tomorrow night?" He laughed, "Sure. I guess." "I need your permission." "Ok." We talked for a while longer and then hung up. It was late but I was wide awake now.

I set up to do an energy healing. During the healing I saw his prostate, it was black. I removed all of the black and infused it with white light. When I went in the second night the prostate looked fine. I was relieved. Ben called me Friday before he went to the hospital. I told him he was fine, not to worry. He said he would call after it was finished and he was home.

It was Monday night before Ben called again. "Sparkie, what the hell did you do?" "Hello Ben, how are you doing?" "I am fine, the doctor went in and nothing was wrong with my prostate, he said it looked like a 30-year old's. Now, What Did You DO?" He was yelling in the phone. I was confused why he would be so mad. "Are you a Voodoo person?" "No, I told you, I am an energy healer. That's all." "That's all huh? Well, don't ever contact me again." "Ok, but why?" "Because I don't want you around me, that's why. There is something wrong with you!" and the line went dead.

I haven't heard from him since that night. I think about him often and wonder why I scared him so badly. Why he wasn't just happy to be healed. Since that time I don't just jump into healing people anymore. I heal the ones that the Whisperers say to heal and I leave the others alone. I had a teacher at school ask me why I didn't heal her. All I could tell her was that I wasn't told to heal her. She looked at me strange and stopped talking to me. So now I rarely talk about healing, until someone tells me of a problem and the Whisperers tell me to ask if I can do energy work on them. When that happens and they are healed, they are grateful and give the appreciation to the All Father where it belongs.

If you are a healer and you have run into people like Ben, listen to your Whisperers. Evidentially, everyone isn't supposed to be healed. This is not our judgement but divine judgement. Remember we are just the hollow bone that the healing energy flows through.

My Engagement Ring Returned

My late husband, Robert Howard Miner, better known as Cappy, passed in 2013. When Cappy left to go to Florida, we were separated and I thought we were divorced in November 2012. But come to find out that wasn't right. (For more information read Cappy's Passing.) It's now 2020.

It had been one of those Saturdays of cleaning up and getting organized, sorting through stuff you really never knew you had. I was getting ready for my daughter, Sarah's coming to the house or at least being able to see her. February 1, a normal Saturday by any definition. I had started out hunting for my watercolor pencils and had found a few but, not the stock that I have. As I walked into my bedroom, I smelled Cappy's cologne. I was thinking that was odd because when he comes to visit, I always smelled his cigars. He smoked 15-20 a day, it was what killed him. I spotted a computer bag that I had been given for the computer that the school had given me. I didn't use it because it was not a very good one and the strap had broken. Humm, wonder what I had put in there. I sat down in the floor and pulled it to me. Cap's cologne was still in the air, actually heavy now. I opened the bag and there were all of my watercolor pencils! YAY! I pulled them out and started sorting them. When I finished that, just on a whim, I turned the bag upside down and shook it, I was pretty sure I had gotten everything out of it. At least everything I could see. Out from the bag fell my emerald engagement ring! I was speechless and tears started to fall down my cheeks. I thought I would never see it again. I picked it up and put it on.

"Thank you for giving this back to me Cappy." His cologne went away and I just sat in the floor looking at that ring.

The backstory to the ring is, when Cappy and I separated, we had several emeralds that had not been put into settings. My ring was part of the emeralds that he got in South America, long before I came on the scene in the late 1990's. It was my Christmas/ engagement ring. I rarely took it off. When he took the boat back to Florida, he also took the emeralds. I totally agreed they were his before me. He asked for my ring. I gave it back to him reluctantly. I had worn it for over 16 years, but his argument was solid and I agreed with it. We had filed for divorce using the same attorney, Ben. It was not till after Cappy died and all of that fiasco started; that I found out that Cap had told Ben that we were getting back together and not to file the paperwork. I never saw him again after he left on the boat. He was really angry with me and didn't want the divorce. No there was never anyone else for me but there were trysts for him and the last one was all I could take. He always said "You can love all kinds of things and people, but you can only be in love with one person Sparkie, for me that person is you."

He would come and walk with Sargie and me after his passing. It was usually our last, late night walk. We would turn the corner from the apartment and I would smell his cigar. The first time I smelled his cigar it was a late at night walk and there was no one around. When you are smoking a cigar at night it is very visible. I assumed it was Cappy, so I started talking to him. We had several long conversations about everything and got the dust settled. At least I thought it was settled. The fact that he came smelling of his cologne today proved to me that he had gotten over all of it and was finally happy. When the ring dropped out he stayed around long enough to see my reaction and then left. You can't live on a small sailboat with someone on the ocean for 16+ years and just dismiss it all. He will always have a very special place in my heart and his ring will be on my finger.

When loved ones pass that you have had problems with; learn to forgive the transgressions here and forget the transgressions. Remember the person for whom they were to you and why you loved them so. Remember the funny times, caring times, and times you will never forget. As long as you remember them, they are still around. It makes their passing easier for both of you.

Bringing Sarah home

6/20/20

Right after Daisy and I went to bed, I heard gun shots. I started counting them as Daisy started shaking. I was holding her so she couldn't get off the bed. I didn't want to be there alone either. 15 shots and the last three were rapidly shot. The first 12 were spaced like, shot, step, shot, step, but the last three were bam, bam, bam. Then nothing. No sirens, nothing. How crazy! I couldn't go to sleep so I started reading The Art of War. A very interesting book. Then about 1 am I sent Gerry a quick message. He's in Scotland. 6 hours difference I thought he might be up. Nope. Ok trying to sleep and finally did.

Last night I had a dream that woke me up. When I woke up I was scared; the same was I stayed scared when I was a child.

Then the dream – I was in a house in a room off of a hallway. I was an adult. I heard a man's voice, rather loud. I quickly went out into the hallway. There the man was coming out of a bedroom saying "Maybe we will get you a mutual home too, like the dog." I was now flying down the hallway. I stopped the man in the hallway, Daddy? He had a smirk on his face. I started smacking him in the chest as I was talking. "Don't you ever say that to him again, ever! You heard me, that's not true, never again, ever."

I walked into the bedroom, a child was laying on his stomach crying with the covers wrapped around him strangely. I sat on the bed and pulled him to me. I hugged him and asked "What happened?" "I had my light on that's why he said it." I was still hugging him "You are never going to go away to anywhere else. Do you understand? You are never going to go away. You will always be with me." He nodded and hung on to me tight.

Then I woke up. Afraid to move, afraid to breathe, the fear of a child hung on me like a blanket I couldn't lift. I started to cry. I have never felt so alone and defeated as an adult. I was that little kid. I didn't know how or why but that little kid was me and I was terrified! I kept wondering if the man would come back.

Then I got hold of myself. I couldn't discern where I was! Oh yes, I remember. I pulled Daisy over to me and I continued to cry. I reached for the light and turned it on. Oh I know, I'm in New Orleans all alone with no one to love me; no one to care. I so miss having someone anyone to grab hold of and tell me its ok. But there isn't anyone. I am all alone in New Orleans in Treme. I wouldn't live anywhere else.

I eventually went back to sleep and when I woke that dream was still rolling around in my mind. I looked around and looked at Daisy. What is wrong with me? Why am I having dreams of being a little kid again and the tears started running down my cheeks. It's now 2 pm and it's not much better. I am not sure what that dream was about but I know it was something I need to deal with. I have a heavy heart and nothing is getting rid of it. I decided to write it out and look at it but that isn't really helping either. I will try some meditation.

I started rewriting stories of the metaphysical things that have happened to me in my lifetime; maybe that's it. Some memories are being stirred up that I haven't dealt with. Not sure. Maybe.

I talked to my daughter Sarah later that Saturday. I shared with her that I had had a bad dream last night.

"I know it was in the wee hours of the morning. You were in my dream. You saved me. Thank you." "Wait what? You had a bad dream too?"

"Maybe we will get you a mutual home like the dog." After she said that I just sat there. Well that explains what she was feeling, but why was she having abandonment issues now? She says everything is fine between her boyfriend and herself.

On Monday I got a phone call from the diagnostic place. They had openings that they could take Sarah early for her imagining. The lady could not get a hold of her. I told her I would try. I called Sarah several times and got no answer. I texted her no answer. I did this for several hours, then I texted her boyfriend. He was in Bowling Green but said he would head back to Franklin where they lived. I suggested her call the nurse and reschedule her appointment for earlier in the afternoon. I texted the nurse and let her know that Bobby was rescheduling Sarah's appointment. Later that Monday I got a text from Sarah that said "I hate my life." I texted her back "Come to New Orleans. Hate your life here." I started to get concerned everything wasn't all right. I texted back and forth with her and then decided to go pick her up. "I'm lonely, you should come visit."

"Ok, give me time to wake up." I started making plans to go to Bowling Green, Kentucky to pick up my daughter. Standing by the dining room table, I said out loud, "How am I going to do this finically?" I picked up my phone and looked at my bank account. I knew what the balance was, I was just making sure I was right. But what I saw shocked me. The balance was much higher than it should have been. I went into details and found that Jefferson Parish Schools had made a deposit into my account! I texted Colin to see what this was all about. He didn't know and he didn't have a deposit in his account. I then texted my friend Billie and asked her what was going on. She said that it was a bonus because I was teaching a critical need area ESL. Oh wow, who knew, not me. I was very grateful for the funds and knew I was supposed to be going to get this child. She was the terrified child in my dream. I am so thankful for Guiding Spirits who talk to me through intuition, dreams, visions, signs, and voices.

I got to Bowling Green at midnight. Picked up Sarah and we went to Motel 8. It was very clean and nice. My daughter looked like she had lost 20+ pounds since March. She had dark circles under her eyes. I should have come sooner, but I had no indication anything was wrong. Wow! She is here with me in New Orleans now. She has been sleeping off and on since we got home Wednesday morning at 2 am. We are now trying to figure out how to transfer her down here legally. I'm positive that it is already worked out for us, just waiting on instructions.

Trust your Spirit Guides. They really do have your back, if you listen.

CPSIA information can be obtained
at www.ICGtesting.com
Printed in the USA
LVHW012346111220
673999LV00007B/81

9 781982 253424